Maryland

in the

CIVIL WAR

Maryland in the Civil War

A House Divided

Robert I. Cottom, Jr.

&

Mary Ellen Hayward

Published by
THE MARYLAND HISTORICAL SOCIETY

Distributed by
THE JOHNS HOPKINS UNIVERSITY PRESS

This book grows out of "Maryland in the Civil War: A House Divided," a permanent exhibit at the Maryland Historical Society which the Anne Arundel County government generously supported.

Copyright © 1994 by the Maryland Historical Society
Printed in the United States of America

Distributed by The Johns Hopkins University Press
2715 North Charles Street
Baltimore, Maryland, 21218

Library of Congress CIP Number 93-078110
ISBN 0-8018-4880-6

Acknowledgements

This volume is the direct result of an exhibition at the Maryland Historical Society funded by Anne Arundel County and the Maryland Humanities Council. The publication has been made possible through the generosity of the Publications Committee of the Maryland Historical Society.

Special thanks, both for the exhibit and this book go to Jeff Goldman for superb copy photography and extraordinary patience; to Laura Rice, Margaret Welch, and Angela Anthony of the Prints and Photographs department, Maryland Historical Society, for indefatigable help in locating images; to private collectors Ross J. Kelbaugh, Ross M. Kimmel, Frederick D. Shroyer, and Daniel Carroll Toomey for generously sharing information and images from their collections; and to the Historical Society of Carroll County, the Frederick County Historical Society, the Maryland State Archives, Hampton National Historic Site, and B'nai B'rith International, all of whom provided previously unpublished materials and extended every courtesy and cooperation. Thanks as well to the Enoch Pratt Free Library and the Peabody Library of the Johns Hopkins University for making available volumes of *Harper's Weekly* and *Frank Leslie's Illustrated Newspaper*. Our gratitude, too, to Kevin Ruffner for sharing with us his important and we hope soon-to-be-published manuscript, "Border State Warriors: Maryland's Junior Officer Corps in the Union and Confederate Armies." Research assistants Catherine Rogers, Elizabeth Naylor, and Mary Beth Paskiewicz of the Maryland Historical Society located images, information, colorful quotations, and long forgotten materials, some not seen for a century or more. We hope we have done their work justice. Any errors are our responsibility.

CONTENTS

$200 REWARD.

Ran away from the subscriber, living eight miles from the city of Baltimore, on the Falls Turnpike Road, on

Friday, the 21st of May, NEGROES RICHARD & NED,

Richard aged about twenty-six years, five feet six or seven inches high, yellowish complexion, small beard, has a scar on his forehead, stutters a little in conversation, but when he is alarmed it is increased considerably : He is straight and well proportioned, except one leg which is a little crooked from having been once broken. His clothing not known, except a new wool hat, a dark grey broad-cloth surtout coat, and a blue uniform United States soldier's coat, both half worn, and two pair of new calf-skin shoes, one pair of which were right and left. Richard ran away from me in 1814; he was then taken up in Pennsylvania, at the house of a man named Gross, (near York Haven,) where he learned the distilling business----It is probable he will return to that state (and will call at Mr. Gross' house, as he left there a watch and some other articles) and engage with a distiller again.

NED, who was decoyed away by Richard, is about twenty years of age, quite black, five feet eight or nine inches high, stout and well formed, has a pleasant countenance, and generally smiles when spoken to, naturally slow in his motions and of an easy quiet disposition, he walks very erect and when in conversation has given himself the habit of spitting through his teeth. He has no particular marks recollected, except a scar on the back of his hand----His clothing like Richard's not particularly known, except a blue cloth coat with long skirts, a pair of greenish pantaloons, both half worn, and an old furred hat---Richard has provided himself with money by robbing Mr. Edmond T. Scarff of 75 dollars the night he ran away, and it is probable they will soon change their dress.

I will give FORTY dollars to any person that will give me information where they are so that I get them again, or ONE HUNDRED DOLLARS for each if brought home, and all reasonable charges paid.

Thomas Johnson.

N. B. They took with them two blankets, blue stripes, commonly called point blankets, 3 1-2 points.

MAY 25, 1819.

"Perry Hall Slave Quarters, with Field Hands at Work." Detail from the oil painting by Francis Guy, c. 1805. Opposite: An 1819 reward notice for fugitive slaves.

Slavery in Maryland

I have no love for America, as such," a powerful, well-spoken former slave told a hissing, cheering assemblage at the American Anti-Slavery Society's meeting in New York in May 1847. "I desire to see it overthrown as speedily as possible and its Constitution shivered in a thousand fragments, rather than this foul curse should continue to remain as now." Frederick Douglass had fled Talbot County, Maryland, in 1838 and settled in Rochester, New York. From there he traveled widely in the antislavery cause, spreading his message of freedom — or sedition, depending upon who was listening — but always he struck at the heart of the moral quandary troubling the eighty-year-old republic.

Like most Americans, Marylanders preferred not to confront the issue. Some eased their consciences with thoughts that the "peculiar institution" in theirs, the northernmost slave state, was milder than in the Deep South. Public opinion, they argued, made the lash less common in Maryland than on sugar plantations in

Louisiana, in the Cotton Kingdom of Alabama and Mississippi, or along the driving, speculative Red River Valley. Douglass would have none of it. Solemnly he reminded Marylanders that there were "certain secluded and out-of-the-way places, . . ." in their state, "where slavery, wrapt in its own congenial darkness, could and did develop all its malign and shocking characteristics, where it could be indecent without shame, cruel without shuddering, and murderous without apprehension or fear." A willful young man, Douglass had once been sent to a "slave-breaker" who beat him regularly until he confessed to being "broken" and turned into a "brute." Moreover, he thundered, what man could tolerate a condition in which he was not his own, in which he might lose family, shelter, food, or property at the whim of another? Slavery had, he concluded, no mild degree.[1]

A few Marylanders listened, but most looked away. A slave state for more than two centuries, Maryland

Frederick Douglass fled from a Talbot County owner to become one of the nation's leading antislavery spokesmen. The portrait is from his book, Narrative of the Life of Frederick Douglass, An American Slave *(Worthy, Near Leeds, England, 1846), which disputed the notion that slavery in the border South was milder than in the Cotton States.*

knew firsthand the evils of slavery — the cries, pleading, and awful silence from places like Austin Woolfolk's slave market, one of several in the area of Pratt, Camden, and Eutaw streets in Baltimore. Slave traders, who bought fine houses and prominent pews, discreetly refrained from advertising in the Baltimore city directories. Nor was there a need; everyone knew who they were. And while public opinion frequently forced the beating of slaves out of sight, Marylanders knew it occurred.

But changes in agriculture steadily altered the nature of slavery in Maryland in the decades before 1860. Tobacco was still a significant cash crop in the southern counties, but more planters and farmers diversified. Fruits, vegetables, hogs, cattle, wheat, and corn required less intensive labor. Farmers could prosper by hiring help only when they needed it. Unable to profit with large numbers of slaves, Marylanders sold some to dealers who took them south (larger numbers were sold in-state) or hired them out to manufacturers, carpenters, and shipwrights. A significant number of slaveowners manumitted slaves in their wills. By 1860 the slave population was but half of what it had been in 1800; there were nearly as many free blacks.

Yet if slavery was slowly dying in the state, Marylanders preferred it should die without undue agitation. Above all they detested abolitionists. When in 1827

"Mistress Overseeing the Plantation." Etching by Adalbert Volck, c. 1860. Volck, a German-born silversmith and proslavery satirist, sought to depict Maryland slavery as a reasonable and efficient institution.

Benjamin Lundy, publisher of *The Genius of Universal Emancipation*, denounced Austin Woolfolk for cursing a black man who was about to be hanged, Woolfolk sought him out and knocked him down. Lundy sued— and received the spiteful award of one dollar. Three years later, William Lloyd Garrison joined Lundy in Baltimore and assailed slave traders in the pages of the latter's paper. Two traders sued for libel and won a fifty-dollar judgment that Garrison refused to pay. Subsequently jailed, Garrison attacked the city and slavery from his cell until embarrassed authorities released him forty-nine days later.[2] Garrison removed himself to Boston and began his own newspaper, the *Liberator*, in January, 1831.

The nation's most outspoken abolitionist had barely left Baltimore when slaves in Virginia's Northampton County rose under Nat Turner and slaughtered thirty-one whites, many of them women and children. Though Turner and his followers were quickly captured and the revolt quelled, the bloodiest slave revolt in American history left the slave states shaken. Like Virginians, who feared not only revolt but, later, invasion by abolitionists from Ohio and Pennsylvania, Marylanders watched their slaves nervously.

The bloody violence of insurrection never came to Maryland, but slavery rested on violence, and Maryland could not escape. The slave cursed by Woolfolk was hanged for his part in the mutiny on the *Decatur*, a slave ship. Frederick Douglass recorded in horrid detail the beatings and tortures inflicted on slaves within his sphere of Talbot County. Then in 1848 Edwin Gorsuch and a small party followed runaways from his Maryland estate into Pennsylvania. Near Christiana, in Lancaster County, they found them. Armed blacks emerged from the cabin in which the fugitives were hidden and opened fire. Gorsuch died in the fusillade.

It was but a prelude to the wrath to come.

"An overseer doing his duty." Benjamin H. Latrobe painted this pastoral scene in 1798.

Men are not *born free and equal in any practical sense of the terms; neither have they any such inalienable rights as . . . right to life, or to liberty, . . . or even to the pursuit of happiness, except so far as it is involved in the pursuit of virtue.*

Rev. E. J. Stearns, *Notes on Uncle Tom's Cabin: Being a Logical Answer to Its Allegations and Inferences against Slavery as an Institution* (Philadelphia, 1853)

An Agonizing Moral Issue

"Flogging the Negro," from The Suppressed Book about Slavery! *(New York, 1864). The book was prepared for publication in 1857 but "never published until the present time."*

Henrietta went over to Mrs. Talbot's this evening for butter and she came back crying and said that there was an awful fuss over at Mrs. Talbot's. She saw a great crowd in the barn yard and Mrs. Talbot standing there. She did not know what it was. So she went near, but soon she ran back for there she saw a poor negro woman stripped bare back, one man beating her with a cowhide, three other men looking on, and that Talbot woman looking to see that it was done right. Henrietta says she never saw such a scene in her life. She said you could hear the strokes of the cowhide and the poor woman's screams were awful. Mrs. Talbot's children were all up at the house crying and one of the other women told Henrietta that Mrs. Talbot was very cruel. I do not know what she was whipped for, but no matter what she did no person has a right to whip his or her fellow creature in that manner, as if they belonged body and soul to them. I am determined never to go to Mrs. Talbot's again and if I can help it never to speak to that fiend in woman's shape again, for if she can stand by and see a fellow creature so beaten, she is no Christian and is not fit company for us. This has put me more against slavery than I ever was. That woman was the mother of 6 children too, and the most valuable slave Mrs. Talbot has.

From the diary of Georgianna Morris, age sixteen, September, 1854, Lutherville, Maryland

Right: By 1847 Frederick Douglass had become a prominent speaker at antislavery meetings. Proslavery Marylanders reacted strongly to his growing national and international acclaim. This tract, published locally in 1847, warned of the dangerous fanaticism of "the runaway slave from Baltimore."

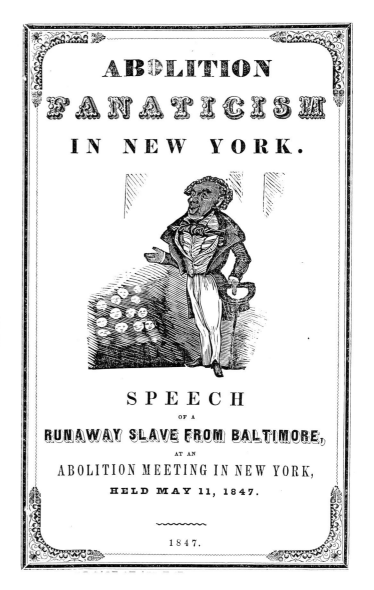

ABOLITION FANATICISM IN NEW YORK.

SPEECH OF A RUNAWAY SLAVE FROM BALTIMORE, AT AN ABOLITION MEETING IN NEW YORK, HELD MAY 11, 1847.

1847.

[Abolition] is the chief cause of the strife that agitates and the danger that threatens our country.

Rev. Henry J. Van Dyke, *The Character and Influence of Abolitionism!* (Baltimore, 1860)

Masters sometimes kill their slaves; husbands sometimes kill their wives; parents sometimes kill their children; but these acts of ferocity occur very rarely; and, when they do, are equally visited with the same condign punishment. In my own State, and I believe in her sister States of the South, the same scorn and public reprobation would fall on the master who would treat his slave with unjust cruelty as would fall upon the husband that would oppress his wife, or the parent who would oppress his child . . .

J. J. Speed, *A Letter from a Gentleman of Baltimore to His Friend in the State of New York on the Subject of Slavery* (Baltimore, 1841)

But it is asked, . . . 'Have you not irritated, have you not annoyed your American friends and the American people rather than done them good?' I admit that we have irritated them. They deserve to be irritated.

Flaming Abolition Speech Delivered by the Runaway Slave, Frederick Douglass, at the Anniversary of the American Anti-Slavery Society, in the Tabernacle, New York, May 11, 1847

"Human Flesh at Auction." From The Suppressed Book about Slavery! *(New York, 1864).*

You talk of freedom? Out for shame!
Your lips contaminate the name.
How dare you prate of public good,
Your hands besmear'd with human
    blood?

From John A. Collins, *The Anti-Slavery Picknick*
(Boston, 1842)

That the Institution of Slavery,
then, is one of the primitive domestic
relations, ordained and established by
the Creator, for wise purposes, and is one
of the best means of promoting the
happiness of the human family, I have
no doubt . . .

J. J. Speed, *A Letter from a Gentleman of Baltimore to His*
Friend in the State of New York on the Subject of Slavery
(Baltimore, 1841)

I am in the prison of a city
which is the scene of a daily
traffic in the persons of men,
women and children, which
is as much more *atrocious*
than the African slave-trade,
as the people are more
enlightened than the savages
of the dark coasts of that
wretched continent. There,
a savage, maddened by
liquor, sells to a white stranger,
captives taken in war from hostile
tribes. Here, native citizens sell
American husbands, wives, sons
and daughters, in cool blood, as a
part of the regular traffic *of this*
Christian city. The traders in
souls ride in their carriages; their
families mingle in its social
circles, and own pews in its
churches,[†] and are very 'respect-
able' men.

[†]Hope H. Salter, *the largest slave-dealer in*
this city, recently bought a pew in the
splendid new Methodist church on Charles
street, much to the annoyance of many of the
worshippers.

J. C. Lovejoy, *Memoir of Rev. Charles T. Torrey,*
Who Died in the Penitentiary of Maryland Where
He Was Confined for Showing Mercy to the Poor
(Boston, 1847)

Harriet Tubman

Born about 1820 near Bucktown in Dorchester County, Harriet Green displayed a childhood resistance to slavery that burst into open defiance when she was fifteen or sixteen. Having followed her master in pursuit of a runaway who was soon cornered in a cabin and captured, she was ordered to bind the man that he might be whipped. Harriet refused and blocked the door as the slave fled. She was severely wounded when the angry owner hurled a piece of iron at the fleeing runaway but missed and struck her forehead. The wound took months to heal and left a deep scar and a permanent injury to her brain that suddenly and sometimes precariously caused her to fall asleep.

Despite her handicap and the resistance of John Tubman, her husband of two years who refused to go along, Harriet escaped from Dorchester County in 1849, moving first to Philadelphia, then to Auburn, New York, and finally to St. Catherines, Canada. She soon joined the Abolition movement and, with the financial support of William Henry Seward and Gerrit Smith, began a series of forays back to her native Dorchester County, where she rescued several of her ten siblings and eventually her aged parents, guiding all to Canada. Before long she was undertaking even more daring raids into the Deep South.

Though only five feet tall she was reportedly as strong as a man and a fast, elusive runner. She also had the physical presence to impose strict discipline on the bands of twenty or thirty runaways she guided as a "conductor" on what soon became known as "the Underground Railroad." When a member of one party lost his nerve and refused to go on, she drew a revolver, pointed it at his head, and coldly commanded: "Move, or die." So notorious and hated in the South was she by the late 1850s that posters advertised rewards for her capture. She dropped off to sleep beneath one — it had no picture, and she was illiterate — but was not caught. Some angry Southerners vowed that when captured she would be burned alive. Still, she managed to outwit pursuers with patience, tactical brilliance, intuition, and luck until in the course of nineteen raids she had brought out between two and three hundred fugitives. Each time she returned to greater applause among

Harriet Tubman (c. 1820–1913), shown here wearing the characteristic scarf with which she covered the terrible scar on her forehead received when she refused to aid in the capture of a runaway.

Abolitionist friends in the North. "For eight or ten years previous to the breaking out of the Rebellion," wrote William Wells Brown, "all who frequented anti-slavery conventions, lectures, picnics, and fairs, could not fail to have seen a black woman of medium size, upper front teeth gone, smiling countenance, attired in coarse, but neat apparel, . . . who, on taking her seat, would at once drop off into a sound sleep."[3]

Her work, and doubtless her life, would have ended in 1859 had it not been for another stroke of fortune. Hearing of her exploits and in need of a black leader for the general slave uprising he intended to begin with his planned raid on Harper's Ferry, John Brown sought her assistance. Brown had first approached Frederick Douglass, but Douglass refused to join the plot, fearing correctly that the plan had no chance to succeed. On meeting Harriet and Wendell Phillips in Boston, an impressed Brown hopefully addressed her as "General Tubman," and she apparently agreed to accompany him on the raid. But the long, exhausting months of her "railroad" work had left her drained. She fell seriously

RUNAWAY.
$150 REWARD!

RANAWAY from the subscriber near Oxford, Talbot co., Md, on May 4th, a likely young negro man, named *PHILIP ADAMS*, about 22 years old.   He is six feet high, round featured and good looking, with copper-colored complection, large feet and awkward in his walk.   His voice is husky in tone, and he hesitates when spoken to.

I will pay the above reward if he is caught out of the State; $100 if caught out of the county, and $50 if caught in the county.   In all cases to be secured in some convenient Jail, so that I can get him.

TENCH TILGHMAN,

May 4th, 1861.   *This was probably the last advertisement ever made in Talbot County of a Runaway negro. S.A.H.*   near Oxford. Md.

Reward poster for a slave who ran away two weeks after the outbreak of war and the arrival of Massachusetts militia on Maryland soil.

ill and was bedridden in New Bedford as Brown impatiently watched the season grow late. When Brown felt he could wait no longer and moved on Harper's Ferry in October, 1859, Harriet was trying to join him and was in New York, on her way to Maryland, when Brown was captured. In April, 1860, she led the bloody attempt to rescue a fugitive slave being held in Troy, New York.

When war broke out, Tubman is said to have followed the first armies moving south. She may well have accompanied Gen. Benjamin F. Butler's force as it moved through Maryland to secure the state and protect Washington. When federals later captured Port Royal,

South Carolina, she organized the Sea Island blacks, served as a nurse in the Port Royal hospital, and in June, 1863, helped organize and lead a raid into the Combahee River region. Clad in a blue jacket, a coarse, striped woolen dress, and a bandanna of the same material as the dress — and probably carrying a rifle — she freed 750 slaves, many of whom immediately enlisted in the Union army. A month later she was among those who buried the dead of the 54th Massachusetts after their fateful assault on Fort Wagner.

Despite her services, Harriet Tubman was never treated well by the government or by white society. She received nothing herself and watched resentfully as black soldiers were offered half the pay of whites. She blamed the president, and later told an interviewer:

> I'm sorry now, but I didn't like Lincoln in those days. . . . You see we colored people didn't understand then that he was our friend. All we knew was that the first colored troops sent South from Massachusetts only got seven dollars a month, while the white got fifteen. We didn't like that. But now . . . I'm sorry I didn't go see Mr. Lincoln.

Her only privilege was the use of military transportation, but after the war, as she journeyed northward to her home in Auburn, a conductor ignored the pass entitling her to ride at half fare. When she resisted, he and two or three male passengers forcibly removed her to a freight car.

Harriet Tubman would live an astonishing forty-eight years after Appomattox, most of them in poverty and in a never-ending fight with the government to get what she claimed as her due — a pension for her role as a military nurse. In 1867 her unfaithful husband John Tubman, who had docilely remained in Maryland slavery and remarried, was murdered on a road near Cambridge. His white assailant was acquitted. Two years later Harriet married Nelson Davis, a black soldier twenty years her junior whom she had met in South Carolina in 1864. Davis died in 1888. Entitled to a widow's pension of eight dollars a month, she survived as best she could, borrowing money to feed the many former slaves who came to live with her, sending money to freedmen's schools in the South, and planning a home for penniless blacks in Auburn. Shortly after she managed to establish such a home — named after John Brown — she moved into it, and there she died, on March 10, 1913. A few hours before her death, according to the Auburn *Citizen*, she motioned two ministers and the few friends with her to come closer to the bedside and quietly directed her own service.

Slaves making their way out of bondage, from The Underground Rail Road *(Philadelphia, 1872).*

I, John Brown am now quite certain that the crimes of this guilty, land: will never be purged away; but with Blood.

John Brown, Charlestown, Va, 2d December 1859

Insurrection!

"John Brown," Harper's Weekly, *November 5, 1859.*

I have only a short time to live — only one death to die, and I will die fighting for this cause. There will be no more peace in this land until Slavery is done for. I will give them something else to do than to extend slave territory. I will carry this war into Africa.

So saying, John Brown of Osawatomie turned east from "Bleeding Kansas." With him came a fiery legacy that would soon rend quiet Maryland.

Born in 1800, this ne'er-do-well farmer and merchant from North Elba in upstate New York early had taken up the antislavery cause, befriending escaped slaves and gaining the financial support of wealthy abolitionists. In 1854–55 several of his sons moved to the Kansas Territory and staked claims a few miles west of Osawatomie, a free-state settlement south of Lawrence on the Marais des Cygnes River. They wrote of the tensions there between settlers from the free states who wanted no slavery in the territory and proslavery elements who formed what they called "Annoyance Associations." Seeing it was there that the battle over slavery would soon be fought, Brown joined them in the fall of 1855.

And a battle it was. Free soil settlers, many of them sponsored by the abolitionist New England Emigrant Aid Society, were intent upon keeping slavery — and blacks — out of the territory. Proslavery settlers, aided by forces from Missouri, were just as intent upon extending slavery into the West. In March, 1855, five thousand Missourians — "enough to kill every God-damned abolitionist in the Territory," they boasted — had crossed the border and forced the selection of a proslavery legislature. That autumn representatives of the free-state majority in Kansas met in Topeka, wrote a defiant constitution, and called for new elections in January. After a bloodless showdown called the Wakarusa War in December, and the murder of a free-state captain during the January elections, open warfare finally broke out on May 21, 1856. Missouri "border ruffians" burned the Free State Hotel, a sturdy brick fortress in Lawrence, a town described as "a piece of New England set down in the prairie." The invaders destroyed several newspapers and burned a number of homes, but only one man was killed. Summoned from Brown's Station near Osawatomie, John Brown and his armed company, the Pottawatomie Rifles, learned en route that the attack was over and that they could be of no help. But Brown noted that six free-state men had died in the recent violence and decided it was time to "strike terror into the hearts of the proslavery people." With four of his sons and two others he turned south toward the handful of proslavery homesteads on Pottawatomie Creek.

A deeply religious man convinced he was acting in God's name, Brown was something of an Old Testament warrior. In addition to rifles, pistols, and knives, his men wore outdated artillery broadswords purchased with funds from the New England Emigrant-Aid Society. Keeping his intentions secret until the last moment, even from his sons, he struck suddenly on May 23, 1856. On that windy night his party descended swiftly on three homesteads, demanding the men of the house and breaking down the doors to get at them. They led the victims — five in all — into the night and hacked them to pieces with broadswords in what Brown deemed biblical vengeance. The Pottawatomie Massacre brought Brown a national reputation variously as a gallant antislavery leader or a murderer and horsethief.

In the fall of 1856, after fighting pitched battles, raiding horses and cattle, and losing one of his sons in a vengeful proslavery attack on Osawatomie, Brown came east and conferred with Thomas Wentworth Higginson, Samuel Gridley Howe (whose wife, Julia Ward Howe, would later write *The Battle Hymn of the Republic*), Theodore Parker, George Luther Stearns, Gerrit Smith, and Franklin B. Sanborn. To these "Secret Six"

he presented a grand plan to strike a great blow against slavery by establishing an army in the Southern mountains and fomenting a general slave uprising across the South.

Brown, who thought regular army troops were lazy and inept, had studied books on guerrilla warfare and was fascinated with the success of small forces operating in the mountains. He also studied the census, marking on a map counties with large slave populations. His planned invasion of the South would begin in the Appalachians, long a favorite route of escaping slaves, whom he presumed would flock to him. Those who would not fight could be sent northward while the more vigorous could take the revolution into Alabama, Mississippi, and South Carolina. But he needed arms, many more than his generous conspirators could supply. The initial blow, therefore, must come against the federal arsenal in the mountains at Harper's Ferry, Virginia. With the arsenal's stock of rifles, and pikes from his abolitionist supporters, he would disappear into the mountains, whence the revolution against slavery could begin.

In the summer of 1859, posing first as "Isaac Smith," a cattle buyer, then as a prospector when boxes of "mining tools" began to arrive, he took up residence at the Kennedy farm, seven miles from the Ferry on the Maryland side of the Potomac. Several of his sons were along — not all agreed to come. A few daring men, white and black, adventurers and idealists, joined him. Some had rescued fugitive slaves, and forty-five-year-old Dangerfield Newby came to free his wife and children in Virginia. Brown drew up a constitution for his "army" and sought help from Harriet Tubman and Frederick Douglass. "Come with me, Douglass," he pleaded when the two men met secretly near Chambersburg in August, 1859. "When I strike, the bees will begin to swarm, and I shall want you to help hive them." But Douglass, who well knew the Southern mind, declined, warning that Virginia would "blow him and his hostages sky-high rather than that he should hold Harper's Ferry an hour."[4]

Brown's band grew until it reached twenty-one in number and, despite hiding upstairs in the farmhouse during the day, could hardly be concealed from his neighbors. Though Brown deceived young Henry Kyd Douglas (later of Stonewall Jackson's staff), who thought

"The Storming of the Engine House by the United States Marines," Harper's Weekly, *November 5, 1859.*

him a sincere old farmer, and though he sent for his daughters to keep up the house and appearances, he was discovered. An old farm woman entered the house uninvited and spotted one of the black "soldiers." Since rumors had begun to circulate regarding his departure from Kansas and what he might be planning next, Brown decided he could wait no longer.

On the chill, drizzly night of Sunday, October 16, Brown with eighteen followers and a wagon filled with pikes and revolvers marched quietly down into Harper's Ferry. At approximately 10:30 they seized the watchman on the sturdy wooden B&O bridge across the Potomac and by midnight had occupied the arsenal, rifle works, and fire engine house. Brown then sent small parties into the nearby countryside in search of slaveholders to use as hostages. One of those seized was a great-grandnephew of George Washington.

In a few hours the town and countryside awoke to their presence. An eastbound B&O train stopped at the bridge, now held by Brown's sentinels. In the ensuing confusion, Brown's men shot dead a free black baggage master, Hayward Sheppard. Immediately alarm bells rang the dreaded signal that an insurrection had begun.

Townspeople and farmers reached for their weapons and rushed to the arsenal. By morning militia from the surrounding counties had arrived, and Brown, who had ignored pleas from some of his men to take the arms and flee into the mountains as planned, was trapped in the engine house with his thirty-odd hostages.

Bars and hotels did a brisk business in liquor as angry townsmen and militia flushed raiders from their isolated posts and savagely gunned them down. One, though captured and made prisoner, was taken to the river, shot in the head, and thrown in the water, where he lay face-up for days. Another, shot on a small islet, became the target of drunken sharpshooters until his riddled body slid into the water. Dangerfield Newby was shot and mutilated in a gutter.

On Monday night a detachment of U.S. Marines arrived along with Col. Robert E. Lee of the 2d Cavalry, who quickly planned a frontal assault on the engine house. On Tuesday morning, as a crowd of two thousand watched, Lt. J. E. B. Stuart, who had served in Kansas in 1856 and instantly recognized Brown, approached the engine house under a flag of truce and demanded the old man's surrender. After looking around at the remainder of his band, including two of his sons — one wounded and dying, the other dead — Brown refused. Stuart jumped aside, and an assault party smashed the heavy doors with sledge hammers. Marines poured into the engine house. Two fell as they bayoneted Brown's men. Lt. Israel Green, who led the assault, thrust his saber at Brown so hard he lifted the old man off his feet, but the blade struck his buckle or a rib and did not run him through. Bleeding and overpowered, Brown was made a prisoner.

A particularly swift trial followed. On October 25, a week after the capture, Virginia governor Henry A. Wise had Brown before a grand jury in Charlestown. Two days later his trial began on charges of murder, inciting a slave revolt, and treason. Brown attended each day, carried into the courtroom on a litter. The court, not surprisingly, found him guilty, and on November 2 sentenced him to hang a month later.

The nation awaited his execution. Southerners girded for an abolitionist invasion from Pennsylvania or Ohio and for anticipated attempts to free Brown. (The Secret Six did plot an escape, but Virginia authorities had found in the Kennedy farmhouse incriminating letters that sent all but Higginson flying from possible arrest.) The wife of one of the men Brown had slain at Pottawatomie wrote to express her delight at the sentence and promised that her surviving son would watch him die. Brown sent forth from his cell eloquent and courageous letters, testimony to his belief in the anti-slavery cause. Some abolitionists grieved at his passing, but not all. "Let no man pray that Brown be spared!" cried Henry Ward Beecher. "Let Virginia make him a martyr!"

On the morning of December 2, 1859, the guard unlocked Brown's cell. He shook hands with his men, admonishing each, "Never betray your friends." Wearing the clothes in which he had been captured, slippers, and an old wide-brimmed hat, he mounted his coffin in the back of a wagon and rode to the gallows erected in a field outside the town. There, fifteen hundred troops, militia, and spectators waited. It was a balmy, late autumn day, and Brown remarked on the beauty of the countryside. He climbed the gallows steps quickly, declined a handkerchief with which to signal the hangman, and stood quietly as the hood covered his eyes. His executioners led him over the trap, but there were delays — a full ten minutes' worth. Brown kept his poise. A professor from the Virginia Military Institute, Thomas J. Jackson, commented on his "unflinching firmness," but in the ranks of the 1st Virginia Regiment one young man thought differently. Contemptuously, John Wilkes Booth looked on as the trap fell.

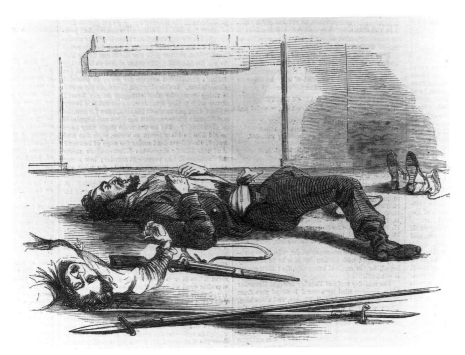

A wounded John Brown lies on the floor of the Harper's Ferry engine house, from Harper's Weekly, *November 5, 1859.*

I live just between the North and the South, hearing both sides of the question and feeling both sides. . . . I do not believe that a State has the right to secede, but when every constitutional mode of obtaining redress is exhausted and when the evil is of a sufficient magnitude, there always remains underneath every constitution and every government that last right of revolution.

McHenry Howard to Francis G. Wood, November, 1860

Election tickets for the four candidates in the presidential race of 1860.

"Bombardment of Fort Sumter by the Batteries of the Confederate States, April 13, 1861." Harper's Weekly, *April 27, 1861.*

A Terrible Choice

Like a boiling reef, the election of 1860 loomed before a foundering American ship of state. A defensive South, freshly angered and shaken by John Brown's raid a few months before, ominously threatened secession as the political parties convened that summer. In Chicago, the six-year-old Republican party nominated a moderate Illinois railroad lawyer who pledged neither to disturb slavery nor to permit its expansion. In Charleston, fiery Southerners leading one branch of a badly splintered Democratic party nominated John Breckenridge, an aggressively pro-slavery candidate. Meeting at the Front Street Theatre in Baltimore (where the floor collapsed beneath them),

the Democratic party's northern wing nominated Stephen A. Douglas, sponsor of the Kansas-Nebraska Act. Douglas's "popular sovereignty" doctrine—letting territorial voters decide the local slavery question—had led to the bloodshed in Kansas. Baltimore then hosted a second convention: the newly created Constitutional Union party pledged to discover a compromise that would at once protect the South and still preserve the Union. Their candidate was the aging John Bell of Tennessee.

Throughout the nation, the campaigns proceeded with more than the usual fanfare and excitement of nineteenth-century American politics. In cities and

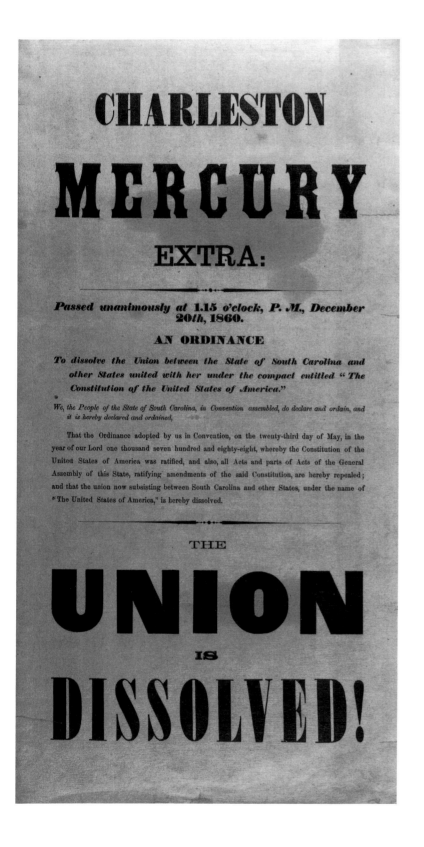

With secession an accomplished fact, comparisons to an earlier American revolution were inevitable.

Eleven states have seceded with unparalleled unanimity from the Union. They desire nothing more than to live at peace and govern themselves. In Heaven's name why not let them depart in peace, why must brothers blood be shed by brothers lances in the most enlightened country and the most enlightened and Christian age?

McHenry Howard, Baltimore,
May 17, 1861

How anyone can compare the revolution down South with the glorious one in which our forefathers rebelled against a government whose very oppressions planted them in America, I am unable to conceive. This tyrannical Lincoln, as you think, is only trying to save us and our nation from eternal ruin.

Frederick A. Shriver to Christopher Columbus Shriver, June 30, 1861

small towns, parks and picnic groves, there were lengthy speeches, shouts, huzzahs. Democratic clubs and Republican "Wide-Awakes" in their tall caps and oil-skin capes paraded by torchlight with drums and vivid transparencies.

As Maryland elections went, 1860 was only a mildly colorful season. Allegany County's Republican Wide-Awakes marched and raised a Lincoln pole. When Democrats chopped it down, its owner raised it again and stood guard with a shotgun. The Southern-leaning Eastern Shore pondered secession. In Baltimore, Democrats assaulted Republicans in the streets and broke up meetings with vegetables, rotten eggs, and epithets. Still, there was nothing like the cannon fire and pitched battles that had marked the city and state elections of 1857–58. Breckenridge narrowly won Maryland with Bell an extremely close second. Douglas received six thousand votes, Lincoln slightly more than two thousand.

Elsewhere, Republicans triumphed over the split Democratic party, and with 38 percent of the vote Abraham Lincoln became president-elect. The South wasted little time. In December a South Carolina convention passed a resolution of secession. A month later, Mississippi, Alabama, Louisiana, Georgia, and Florida followed.

In its 1860 session the Maryland legislature, apprehending future events, had resolved to cast its lot "with her sister states of the South and abide their fortune to the fullest extent" should the dissolution of the Union actually come to pass. But the legislature met every two years and was not scheduled to convene again until 1862. The call for a special session, in which an ordnance of secession might be passed, had to come from the governor.

A Southern sympathizer and cartoonist, Baltimore dentist Johann Adalbert Volck pictured Lincoln skulking through the city on his way from Springfield to Washington, afraid of a rumored mob attack on his train.

As it happened Thomas Holliday Hicks, although an Eastern Shoreman, was not disposed to hastily set in motion the process by which Maryland might leave the Union. Despite receiving requests and emissaries from Alabama, Mississippi, and South Carolina to do so, Hicks remained adamant. Maryland, he responded irritably, was not about to convene her legislature "at the bidding of South Carolina." Though armed men

I hope Uncle Sam (or rather now Uncle Abe) will give the seceding boys a good sound drubbing. The Constitution and the laws must be sustained.

Jacob Englebrecht, Frederick, April 11, 1861

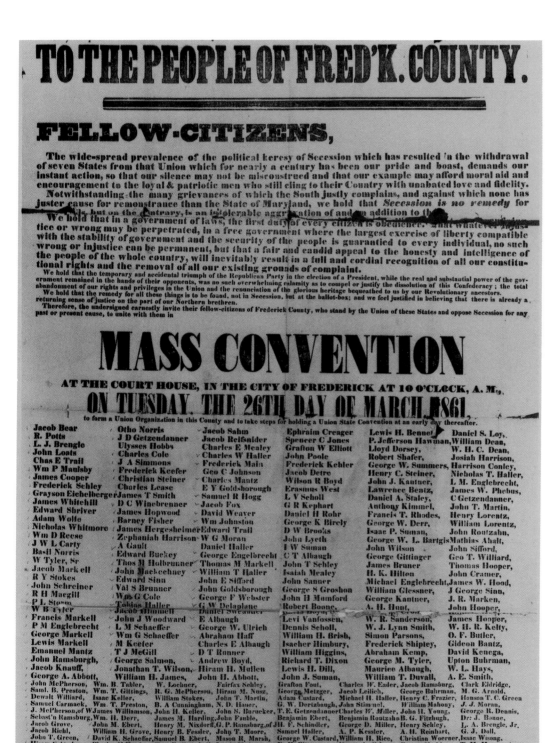

In the turbulent spring of 1861, while the country anxiously waited to see whether Virginia and Maryland would join the Confederacy, Northern and Southern causes gathered support in public meetings throughout the state. In Frederick loyal Union men signed their names to this broadside calling for a rally in March. Historical Society of Frederick County.

sporting blue secession cockades drilled throughout the state, Hicks would not be moved. Mississippi, he noted when the state seceded, had "gone to the devil." In February he appointed representatives to attend a conference of border-state moderates in Washington, but tensions only worsened. Texas, North Carolina, and Tennessee departed the Union.

Then, on April 15, 1861, gunners wearing the uniform of the new Confederate States of America opened fire on Fort Sumter in Charleston harbor, a federal property President Lincoln refused to surrender. Lincoln, who had passed secretly through heavily secessionist Baltimore in February amid fears of an assassination plot, and who had vainly pleaded in his inaugural for reason on all sides, now called on the states to raise 75,000 volunteers to put down the rebellion. Hicks rushed to

"The Boston Regiments Embarking for Washington in the Jersey City Cars." Harper's Weekly, *May 4, 1861.*

THE MASSACRE AT BALTIMORE.

For Northerners, as well as Marylanders with strong Union sentiments, the Pratt Street riot represented an outrageous act of mob violence against federal troops. Graphic depictions of the incident, which resulted in the first bloodshed of the war, appeared in more than a dozen Northern newspapers and periodicals and in the foreign press.

Left: "The Massacre at Baltimore." Hand-colored lithograph by E. B. and E. C. Kellogg, 1861.
Below: "The Lexington of 1861." Hand-colored lithograph by Currier & Ives, 1861. The title refers to the fact that the first shots of the Revolutionary War were fired against Massachusetts soldiers at Lexington and Concord.

The outbreak of April 19th was not a return to mob law as Northern papers say. The roughs are unionists. It resulted from the irrepressible indignation of the people at seeing armed men pass over our soil to subjugate our brethren of the South.

McHenry Howard to Francis G. Wood, May 17, 1861

THE LEXINGTON OF 1861.

The Massachusetts Volunteers fighting their way through the Streets of Baltimore, on their march to the defence of the National Capitol April 19, 1861 Hurrah for the Glorious 6th

Washington to confer with the president, who assured him that Maryland troops would be used exclusively to protect Washington and defend federal property within the state. Hicks warned the administration that Baltimore, through which most rail traffic from the North must pass, had a strong and explosive secessionist bent. He then left Washington for that troubled city and on April 18, amidst a howling mob, issued a plea for peace and union.

But events moved too quickly. While Hicks looked warily over the hostile crowd, a regiment of Pennsylvania volunteers changed trains a few blocks away largely without incident. (One nervous trooper, eyeing the bystanders, dropped his musket and shot himself in the leg. He was taken in and nursed by a young, and, it was said, very pretty Baltimore woman.) The following day another regiment of twelve hundred unarmed volunteers arrived at the President Street station from Philadelphia.

If the Pennsylvanians have been forgotten, not so the troops in the first ten cars of that train on the Philadelphia, Wilmington, and Baltimore Railroad. These were the 6th Massachusetts Volunteer Militia, armed, smartly uniformed, well-drilled, and nearly seven hundred strong. Hailing from Lexington and Concord, they prided themselves in their history and in being the first real armed body to answer the president's call. They had received their flag on Boston Common. In New York they had staged a grand parade, and the previous night in Philadelphia leading citizens had offered their officers a sumptuous dinner. Now, at 10:30 on the morning of April 19, 1861, a few miles from Baltimore, the 6th received orders to load its rifles. Baltimore was not only secessionist, it bore the fearful reputation of a "mobtown."

By virtue of a city ordinance enacted during the great railroad boom of the 1830s and 1840s, Baltimore permitted no locomotives to run through the city. Trains coming south down the Northern Central stopped at Bolton Hill station. The B&O terminated at Camden yards, the Philadelphia, Wilmington, and Baltimore at President Street. To proceed, cars from one train were hitched to teams of horses and drawn along tracks through the city to the next station. The 6th Massachusetts would be hauled from President Street across the Jones Falls bridge and along the Pratt Street water-front to the B&O's Camden Station, a journey of a little more than a mile.

One after another the cars, each bearing a company of about seventy men, were hitched up for the long pull. Inside, the men watched nervously as bystanders began to gather. Word of their coming had preceded them, and the small crowd at the station grew quickly. The cars moved into the narrow canyon of Pratt street. Between the buildings the men glimpsed secession flags streaming atop mastheads in the harbor. The crowd hooted insults, and a few waved pistols or threw stones at the cars, but the first companies crossed to Camden Station without incident.

The tension mounted. Angry men dropped an anchor on the tracks, then a cartload of sand, blocking the last three cars. Some in the crowd shot their pistols into the air. One company fought its way through to Camden Station. With the mob growing ever larger and more raucous, the remaining volunteers—four companies—detrained and formed for the march. A citizen bearing the new Confederate Stars and Bars moved at their head, forcing them to parade behind the secession flag. Bystanders howled with delight and derision. A few darted at the troops to wrestle away a flag or rifle. More shots cracked. Officers gave the order to double-quick and the men moved off at a trot. Missiles began to rain on them from the windows overhead, and from their flanks came heavy paving stones. The troops staggered; four fell with mortal wounds, and stricken soldiers crawled into doorways where compassionate citizens hid and sheltered them. The 6th Massachusetts opened fire.

Accounts differ wildly about what happened next. Baltimoreans in nearby homes claimed they heard very little, and a private in the 6th bravely wrote his mother that the action was vastly exaggerated. A Massachusetts major later likened it to a pitched battle, though he would never fight in any during the war.[1] Nevertheless, when the smoke cleared a dozen citizens lay dead, an unknown number were wounded.

Though Baltimore's antislavery mayor, George William Brown, had briefly joined the troops in a vain effort to control the crowd, and though a police line mustered by Marshal George Kane eventually rescued the troops from the mob at Charles Street, the melee instantly took on overtones which were to affect Maryland for the rest

*But remember that it was the sixth
regiment that killed the first secessionist.*

Pvt. Lyman Van Buren Furber, 6th Massachusetts
Volunteer Militia, April 23, 1861

*Bring your men by the first train.
. . . Streets red with Maryland blood;
send expresses over the mountains of
Maryland and Virginia for the riflemen
to come without delay. Fresh hordes
will be down on us tomorrow. We will
fight them and whip them or die.*

Police marshal of Baltimore, George P. Kane to
Bradley T. Johnson, April 19, 1861

*A small body of influential, honorable,
and sincere members [of the state legisla-
ture] were opposed to hasty action. They
dallied and delayed and lost a week. A
week in war, never to be recovered. A
week in Revolution — a century in the
tranquil current of civil affairs.*

Bradley T. Johnson, *Memoir of the
First Maryland Regiment, 1881*

*It seems to me, Old Lincoln ought to
have better sense, than try to coerce the
South. We can never do it. . . . The
old tyrant I wish he had never been
born, or since he is; I wish that he were
now in Heaven— instead of where he is.*

C. C. Shriver to Frederick A. Shriver, June 6, 1861

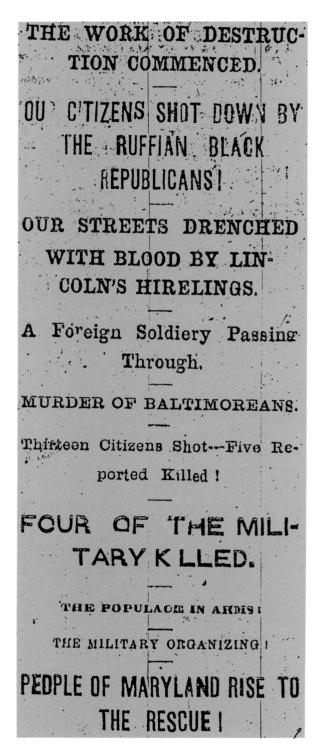

Baltimore's pro-Southern newspapers loudly decried the events of
April 19, 1861, when soldiers from the 6th Massachusetts regi-
ment fired into a local mob, resulting in casualties on both sides.
After federal occupation of the city in May, military authorities
suppressed no fewer than nine newspapers. Only the loyal
American, *the* Clipper, *and the discreet* Sun *remained in publica-
tion throughout the conflict. This clipping is from the* Baltimore
Republican, *April 19, 1861.*

"The New Jersey Troops Crossing the Chesapeake Bay, in Sixteen Propellers, on Their Way to Washington. From a Sketch by an Officer of the Expedition." From Frank Leslie's Illustrated Newspaper, *May 18, 1861. After the Pratt Street riot President Lincoln agreed not to send federal troops through Baltimore. Instead, they sailed from New Jersey to Annapolis, where Gen. Benjamin F. Butler and eight hundred men of the 8th Massachusetts had arrived on April 21.*

of the war. Despite the fact that one 6th Massachusetts soldier could tell his mother not to worry about "the skirmish we had at Baltimore" because he was "neither hurt nor frighten,"[2] Southerners called the "Battle of Baltimore" a heroic resistance to northern tyranny. Northerners labeled it "The Lexington of 1861" and vowed henceforth to "go through Baltimore, or die!" In twenty minutes Southern sympathizers and waterfront thugs had transformed a divided city into a traitorous hotbed in Northern eyes, and neither President Lincoln nor a series of Northern generals would disagree.

In Baltimore nerves were strained to the breaking point. To prevent further troop movement — and violence — Mayor Brown ordered the burning of railroad bridges north of the city. Armed Marylanders forced a Pennsylvania regiment to turn back at Cockeysville. When an over-eager junior officer at Fort McHenry threatened to train his guns on the Washington Monument, a Baltimorean replied that if he did, "there will be nothing left of you but your brass buttons to tell who you were." Angry citizens briefly considered taking possession of the fort but thought better of it.

Even as the 6th Massachusetts was clattering south on the B&O, firing out the windows (and killing an innocent farmer near Relay House), the 8th Massachusetts Regiment of volunteers under the command of

For some days all, throughout the State nearly, believed her virtually withdrawn from the Union during that unfortunate affair of April last, at that time I resigned and offered my services to Gov. Hicks 'to assist in repelling any invasion of her soil by our Northern enemies,' such was the light in which every person I met, viewed it. . . . it was not considered the act of a mob until some days after the occurrence, then the change to Union was as sudden as from Secession to Union.

Franklin Buchanan, June 26, 1861

"The Uprising at the North, Men of the 8th Mass. Repairing the Railroad Bridges from Annapolis to Washington, May 1861." Wood engraving from Harper's Pictorial History of the Great Rebellion *(New York, 1866–68). Butler's men quickly repaired bridges on the railroad to Washington.*

Benjamin Franklin Butler was steaming south down the Chesapeake. Though he had been the gubernatorial candidate on the Breckenridge ticket in Massachusetts, Butler was all business when Lincoln called for volunteers. "When we come from Massachusetts," he told a South Carolinian, "we will not leave a single traitor behind, unless he is hanging upon a tree."[3] Learning in Philadelphia of the Baltimore riot and burned bridges, Butler took the train as far as Perryville at the mouth of the Susquehanna, commandeered the railroad ferry *Maryland*, and soon landed at Annapolis. He quickly took possession of the Naval Academy, offered to protect the white populace against the threat of a non-existent slave revolt, and began repairing the tracks of the Annapolis and Elk Ridge Railroad.

Washington was no longer undefended ("Why don't they come!" an anxious Lincoln was overheard to say as he peered out a White House window just before the 6th Massachusetts arrived), but it still might be cut off if Maryland seceded. On April 22, Governor Hicks finally called the special session of the legislature Maryland secessionists needed to take the state out of the Union, but with Butler occupying Annapolis Hicks scheduled the meeting in heavily Unionist Frederick. The General Assembly met on April 26 and coldly took note of a written invitation from Virginia—which had

Balt. Co. American EXTRA.

TOWSONTOWN, MD.

SATURDAY EVENING, APRIL 20, 1861.

☞ Civil War is in our midst! A riot has occurred between soldiers from the North and the citizens of Baltimore, and unarmed men have fallen beneath the musket shots of soldiers from another State. We have stood long by the UNION FLAG —we have contended thus far beneath its folds, but now we must coincide with Governor Hicks and Mayor Brown, as well as with the sentiments of the people of the entire State, in saying that Northern troops shall not pass unharmed through the State of Maryland, for the purpose of subjugating the South. Northern troops are now, it is said, marching to Washington, intending to *force* themselves through Maryland, and we can but say to our people, respond to the call issued by the Governor, and defend your State.

It is said that Government troops who came as far as the Gunpowder, on the Philadelphia Rail-Road, were prevented from proceeding by the bridge being destroyed, and that they are now marching on foot towards Baltimore.

The Baltimore County Horse Guards, of this place, has been ordered out, and manfully are they responding. They are now gathering, and will march before the going down of the sun.

The "Towson Guards" have not yet received orders, but are momentarily expecting them.

All is excitement here, and, with a few exceptions, all appear to be of one mind.

On the N. C. R. R., the bridges over Western Run and Beaver dams, near Cockeysville, and several bridges near the city, including the iron bridge at the Relay House, have been destroyed, to prevent the transportation of government troops from the North.

The riot in Baltimore proved to be an emotional crucible in the North. Here, on April 24, 1861, at Tammany Hall in New York City, the "Billy" Wilson Zouaves swear allegiance to the flag and pledge to "Go Through Baltimore or Die." From The Soldier in Our Civil War: A Pictorial History of the Conflict, 1861–1865 *(New York, 1887).*

I just now saw up on Lombard St, a company from Maine. They are passing . . . at double quick time, as though they were needed down in Va. [Y]ou ought to see a big Company like 1000 men make — they fill the streets for about four squares and the clatter of their feet and the noise of the crowd following is quite exciting. This company had a pretty good band with them, and played as they marched poor fellows a good many of them will never return I am sure. Tis by George an awful sight to see so many men with muskets, marching down to kill a fellows best friend.

C. C. Shriver to Frederick A. Shriver,
June 6, 1861

Two days after the Pratt Street riot this group of small shopkeepers in the Fells Point section of Baltimore posed at a studio on South Broadway to show their support for the U.S. flag.

Early in May Union general Benjamin F. Butler occupied the B&O Railroad junction at Relay, eight miles southwest of Baltimore, with troops from the 6th Massachusetts and 8th New York. The soldiers set up camp, planted two large cannon on a nearby hill, and prepared themselves should Confederate forces attempt to advance on Washington from Harper's Ferry. They were now also in a position to block the flow of supplies and recruits to Harper's Ferry, where a Confederate Maryland regiment was organizing. Maryland State Archives (Robert G. Merrick Collection) MSA SC 1477–4826.

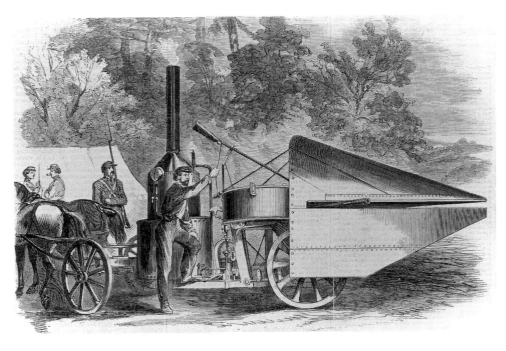

Railroad-car builder, inventor, and wealthy Maryland secessionist Ross Winans (above) built to sell to the Confederate government a steam-powered artillery piece said to be capable of firing five hundred rounds per minute. The gun was en route to Harper's Ferry by rail when Butler's troops intercepted it at Ellicott's Mills and took it to Relay, where it became a great curiosity. The inventor had time to make off with some of its essential components before the gun was captured, and it was never fired. Winans was arrested and incarcerated at Fort McHenry until his release later that summer. Frank Leslie's Illustrated Newspaper, *May 18, 1861.*

not yet seceded — to join the Confederacy. The senate announced it did not possess the authority to consider secession, and despite secessionists' protests, the legislature adjourned.

Lincoln clinched the matter on April 27 by suspending the writ of habeas corpus all along the line from Washington to Philadelphia. Military authorities could

Gen. Benjamin F. Butler, a lifelong Democrat, supported John Breckenridge in the election of 1860.

now arrest and hold resisters without a civil trial. On May 6 Butler occupied Relay House on the B&O eight miles south of Baltimore and cut the route by which Baltimoreans were shipping supplies to the South. He further annoyed Marylanders by warning they should not think of poisoning his troops lest he incite a slave revolt against them. For good measure he announced he could put an armed soldier in any house he chose.

A week later the flamboyant Massachusetts politician-general decided on his own to occupy Baltimore. He first sent a staff captain into the city disguised as an organ grinder. The captain wandered the streets, noting the absence of hostile troops and the presence of a large stock of gunpowder intended for Southern use. At dusk on the evening of May 13, Butler's train rolled into Camden Station just as a thunderstorm broke. Lightning flashed in a darkening sky and gusty winds blew rain in their faces as the men marched through the deserted streets and located the heights of Federal Hill. The military occupation of Baltimore, which would last throughout the war, had begun.

Butler moved into Baltimore during a thunderstorm about dusk on May 13 and occupied Federal Hill with five hundred men of the 6th Massachusetts, the same regiment involved in the April 19 riot. The next day he issued a proclamation prohibiting any action hostile to the federal government. Enraged that Butler had acted without consulting him, Union commander Gen. Winfield Scott relieved Butler from command the following day, but Baltimore would remain under military occupation for the duration of the war. In 1862 troops under Butler's command occupied New Orleans, where a similar independent edict concerning treatment of the women of that city quickly earned him the sobriquet, "Beast."

Glory Hallelujah, gentlemen, we are safe!

Enoch Pratt, hardware merchant, May, 1861

We can no longer mince matters with these desperate people.
I concur in all you have done.

Gov. Thomas H. Hicks to Gen. Nathaniel P. Banks,
Commander of Union troops in Baltimore,
September 20, 1861

After Butler quietly occupied Federal Hill on the night of May 13, 1861, various federal units were stationed there until the end of the war. Baltimoreans who favored the Southern cause viewed this military occupation as brutal oppression. Those who wished Maryland to remain in the Union looked upon the federal presence as their safeguard or deliverance from the threat of being forced out of the Union by secessionist elements. These photographs, dated to the fall of 1862 through the identification of vessels in the harbor, show a gun crew from the 5th New York Heavy Artillery posing in the fortifications. Peale Museum, Baltimore City Life Museums.

Overleaf: On July 2, 1861, Union troops occupied strategic locations in Baltimore, including Battle Monument Square, where they camped for a week. William Weaver, a local photographer who worked on occasion for Harper's Weekly, *made this photograph for the illustrated newspaper to copy in the form of a wood engraving. It is the only known photograph of soldiers in the streets of Baltimore during the Civil War. Ross J. Kelbaugh.*

General: The passage of any act of secession by the legislature of Maryland must be prevented. If necessary, all or any part of the members must be arrested. Exercise your own judgement as to the time and manner, but do the work efficiently.

Simon Cameron, Secretary of War, to Gen. Nathaniel P. Banks, September 11, 1861

Gen. Benjamin Butler's occupation of Federal Hill visibly ended any pretense of Maryland independence or neutrality. A prisoner of geography, the state was simply too important for the Union to lose. President Lincoln took no chances. Unknown to Marylanders, the administration had quietly planned for every contingency, even to "the bombardment of their cities" should Maryland attempt to secede. With troops soon encamped throughout Baltimore and its outskirts, and troop trains able to freely move through to Washington, it remained for the federal government to ensure the loyalty of the state's population.

Despite the legislature's rejection of secession, all through the spring and summer of 1861 strong talk and Southern sentiments abounded in Baltimore, Southern Maryland, and on the Eastern Shore. Baltimore mer-chants had defiantly (and profitably) shipped military supplies to the Confederacy until Butler cut the line at Relay, but his vigilant sentries could not stop young men who eased quietly across the Potomac by the hundreds to put on Confederate gray. In Richmond, Charlottesville, and Harper's Ferry they drilled with the bayonet and spoke angrily of the despot's heel on their beloved Maryland. Newspapers, legislators, and magistrates railed at coercion, and citizens resentful of occupation angrily displayed the Confederate colors, red and white.

While many Unionist Marylanders found reason to rejoice with merchant Enoch Pratt at the security provided by military rule — Butler announced that he would not interfere with loyal men or their property, only that he would enforce federal and state laws — not all

As part of his program to keep Maryland in the Union, President Lincoln authorized the arrest (and imprisonment at Fort McHenry) of those state and local leaders known to have secessionist sympathies. Union troops arrested Police Marshal George P. Kane late in June, finding hidden at his headquarters caches of arms thought to be intended for secessionists' use. In an old back building of City Hall, troops found four cannon, half a ton of shot, eight hundred rifle-ball cartridges, and four hundred-weight of ball; in Kane's office and in the floors and ceiling, pistols, 250 muskets, and rifles. The wood engraving is from Frank Leslie's Illustrated Newspaper, *July 13, 1861.*

James Ryder Randall, a Baltimore native teaching in Louisiana, read with horror in the New Orleans Delta *the list of civilian casualties after the Pratt Street riot. Among the names of the mortally wounded appeared (incorrectly) that of Randall's Georgetown College roommate, Francis X. Ward. Unable to contain his sorrow and indignation at Maryland's fate, Randall wrote a poem. Published three days later in Louisiana and soon set to music as "Maryland, My Maryland," the rousing anthem became a rallying cry for pro-Southern Marylanders and later a favorite of Confederate troops.*

found the federal government's idea of security appealing. Gen. Winfield Scott, angry with Butler for moving into Baltimore and claiming it was "a God-send that it was without conflict of arms," replaced the Massachusetts politician on May 15 with Gen. George Cadwalader. Cadwalader held the reins of military command in Maryland only for a month, but it was long enough to secure for himself a small place in history for defying the Chief Justice of the Supreme Court in the matter of one John Merryman.

With Lincoln's suspension of the writ of habeas corpus along military lines leading to Washington, it fell to the State Department to make arrests of disloyal persons important enough to present a danger to the republic. From the outbreak of hostilities in April, 1861,

until February, 1862, when responsibility for arrests was given to the War Department, 166 Marylanders felt Secretary of State William Henry Seward's heavy hand. At least they assumed it was Seward who ordered the arrests from his office in Washington. So infamous was his reputation that, according to a widely circulated story, he told the British ambassador that he could ring a little bell on his desk and arrest a citizen anywhere in the United States. Could even Queen Victoria do that, Seward asked. In fact, the State Department spent much of its time trying to find out just why local or military authorities had arrested numerous persons in Maryland and elsewhere, but the story of "Seward's little bell" stuck.[4]

One of those arrested in the heated days of May, 1861,

A New York newspaper pictured a "secesh" Baltimore belle parading before occupying federal troops in a dress sporting the Confederate "stars and bars" late in the summer of 1861. Her cocky demeanor suggested to Northern readers that Baltimore remained a hotbed of secessionist sentiment. The engraving, as it appeared on the cover of Harper's Weekly, *September 7, 1861, was entitled, "A Female Rebel in Baltimore—An Everyday Scene."*

Below: "Searching for Arms," copperplate engraving by Adalbert Volck, probably made in 1861. Volck's rabidly anti-Union sentiments, expressed in political cartoons and caricatures, circulated surreptitiously throughout the war years. Using the pseudonym "V. Blada," he sold engravings to "subscribers," somehow managing to produce four volumes of "War Sketches" in the tightly controlled atmosphere of occupied Baltimore. Here he satirized Union occupation commander Gen. John A. Dix's proclamation banning the flying of Confederate flags in Baltimore. Federal soldiers search a young lady's bedroom to find the tiny flag she has hidden while others hold an angry father at bay in the door.

Opposite: In September, 1861, Gen. John A. Dix took command of federal troops stationed in Baltimore and immediately forbade display of the Confederate colors, red and white. This broadside, making great fun of Dix's order, appeared on September 4 and was widely circulated. Songs lampooning Dix also made their way to the streets.

Chief Justice of the Supreme Court Roger Brooke Taney lectured Lincoln, Seward, and the military officials in Baltimore on the dangers and limits of martial law.

was John Merryman, owner of "Hayfields" north of Cockeysville and past president of the Maryland State Agricultural Society. Merryman also led a troop of cavalry, the Baltimore County Horse Guards, and under orders from worried public authorities burned the Northern Central Railroad's bridges north of the city on the night of April 19. At 2 o'clock on the morning of May 25, he was seized at his home and thrown into Fort McHenry, whence his lawyers the following day presented a petition for a writ of habeas corpus in the federal circuit court.

Presiding over that court in the old Masonic Hall on St. Paul Street was no one other than Maryland native Roger Brooke Taney, aging Chief Justice of the Supreme Court. Claiming that he had been "preserved for this occasion," Taney ordered General Cadwalader to bring Merryman before him or show reason why he should not be released. Cadwalader refused, whereupon Taney delivered a blistering lecture on civil rights to everyone involved in military arrests—particularly Seward and Lincoln. The opinion, *ex parte Merryman*,

denounced military rule and military commissions presuming to try civilians and warned of dire consequences to come. Cadwalader ignored him, as did federal authorities, and Merryman remained in his cell. (On July 4 he would be interviewed by Secretary of War Simon Cameron and sometime later released.)

On June 11 Gen. Nathaniel Preston Banks of Massachusetts replaced Cadwalader, promptly arrested the police marshal, George P. Kane, in the middle of the night, and suspended the police board. On disbanding, the police board dismissed the police force, and Banks appointed Col. John R. Kenly of the newly formed 1st Maryland Infantry encamped at Mt. Clare as Provost-Marshal of the city. Kenly brought in four hundred soldiers to replace the police, but he had little stomach for the job and asked to be relieved after two weeks. Banks, too, was soon relieved, replaced by Gen. John Adams Dix on July 23.

Dix brought to Baltimore a mixture of apprehension and methodical energy that, when fully applied, brought the reality of occupation to every street and neighbor-

Gen. Dix's PROCLAMATION

Know all men by these presents: that I, John L. Dix, (no relation to the rebel "Dixie") knowing that the feeling excited in the breasts of our brave Union army by the combination of colors known as red, white and red, are by no means agreeable, do hereby, by virtue of the authority vested in me, by His Majesty Abraham 1st, require and command all police officers of the city of Baltimore in the pay of His Majesty's government to suppress and cause to disappear all substances, whether in the heavens above, or in the earth beneath, or in the waters under the earth, bearing the said combination of rebel colors. All babies having red, white and red stockings on will be sent to Fort Lafayette. All houses built of red brick and white mortar, must be removed, or painted red, white and blue, in alternate stripes. All water-melons must be painted blue on the rind; and all mint candy, and barber's poles so colored are forbidden. All red and white cows are required to change their spots or take the oath of allegiance. Red and white variegated flowers must be altered to include blue. All white persons having red hair and moustaches or whiskers are hereby warned to have the one or the other dyed blue. No sun-rises or sun-sets which exhibit such combinations will be permitted, on pain of suppression. Persons are forbidden to drink red and white wines alternately. His Majesty is, however, graciously pleased to make an exception in favor of red noses, these last being greatly in vogue among Federal officers, and additional *lustre* having recently been shed upon such noses, by one of my former predecessors in this command.

Done at the Baltimore Bastile, this 4th day of September, the 1st year of Abraham's glorious and peaceful reign.

(Signed),   JOHN L. DIX, Maj. Gen.

A young man, who gave the name of John Potter, was arrested yesterday afternoon by officer Blaney, charged with hurrahing for Jeff Davis. He is also accused of having lately returned from Richmond, Virginia. Last night he was sent to Fort McHenry, by order of provost marshal Dodge.

Baltimore Sun, May 24, 1862

hood of the city. Aware of Baltimore's geographic importance to the safety of Washington and afraid that rebellion might rear its head on any corner of Baltimore's historically inflammatory streets, Dix acted swiftly and surely, if not popularly. Seeing that Fort McHenry was vulnerable to attack by land, he strengthened and reinforced it. He also undertook the construction of scientific fortifications on Federal Hill and heavy encampments at Patterson Park, the McKim and Steuart mansions, and Potter's Race Course. Thinking that five thousand troops were not enough to ensure Baltimore's loyalty, he called for reinforcements. To remove the temptation of riot, he forbade the display of Confederate red and white, or the sale of Confederate envelopes or song sheets, all of which were legal in more secure Northern states.

Dix was not squeamish about using military arrests to control Maryland civilians, but he was careful on two important counts. He refused to search private homes, though Unionists were eager to find the "Winans cache" of concealed Southern weapons supposedly hidden in a nunnery, and he insisted that arresting officers present a good case. "I am suspicious of charges against individuals unless they are well supported," he wrote Secretary Seward on October 5, 1861. "Two men were arrested and charged with open acts of hostility only to find . . . [they were] consistent and active Union men." Four months later he complained of "persons arrested by military officers who had been overlooked . . . lying in prison for months without any just cause."[5]

The use of military authority and arrests, never entirely popular even among staunch Maryland Unionists, reached its highest points of controversy during Dix's command. In September, 1861, military authorities turned back pro-Southern, and, it was feared, secessionist Maryland legislators on their way to Frederick for a meeting of the General Assembly. Thirty-one were eventually arrested, as were Mayor George William Brown and former governor Thomas G. Pratt. Inconclusive evidence points to Lincoln or Seward as having suggested the arrests, and Gen. George B. McClellan, commander of the Army of the Potomac, knew of them beforehand. In May, 1862, Judge Richard Bennett Carmichael, an outspoken opponent of military authority, was dragged from his bench in the circuit court at Easton, pistol-whipped, and thrown into Fort McHenry. Anger at the ruthless manner in which Carmichael had been treated followed Dix until he was replaced in July by John E. Wool, who proved even less popular among Marylanders. Wool went so far as to denounce Gov. Augustus Bradford for not being sufficiently loyal and presided over a great wave of arrests in August and September of 1862, when the War Department assigned provost-marshals to every state with instructions to fall hard on any who made disloyal statements or who interfered with recruiting. In the months and years that followed, the household searches and seizures that Dix had foresworn did take place, and women as well as men found themselves imprisoned.

Crime, Court-Martial, and Execution

Military law could fall as heavily on soldiers as on civilians in an occupied city, particularly in an army composed of undisciplined, sometimes unruly volunteers. On the afternoon of September 10, 1861, at Camp Carroll, Pvt. Joseph Kuhne, Company F, 2d Maryland Infantry, got into an altercation with Lt. J. David Whitson, during which Kuhne shot Whitson in the back and killed him. Taken to Fort McHenry and tried for murder, a court-martial sentenced Kuhne to hang.

The first military execution to be held in Baltimore, of a Union soldier and not a Southern sympathizer, provided a colorful spectacle to an excited city. At 10:30 A.M. on the appointed day, residents in every quarter heard "martial music and the heavy tread of soldiery, with cavalry and artillery" as troops from the various encampments convened on Fort McHenry. Civilians, too, flocked to the site of the execution but were prevented from entering. Newspaper correspondents inside satisfied the public's curiosity in grisly detail.

By noon all the military had reached the parade ground at Fort McHenry and formed a hollow square within the enclosure. The gallows was erected near the centre of the ground, and presented to the beholder a fearful sign of recompense for violating the law of God and man by depriving another of life.

Thousands of citizens had congregated outside the enclosure, but a strong guard prevented them from advancing nearer to the scene of execution.

Shortly after twelve o'clock there emerged a wagon from the gateway of the fort guarded by a strong military force. The condemned man was in the wagon, and the procession moved with slow and solemn tread towards the dread instrument of death, while the accompanying band played the "Dead March." On reaching the gallows Kuhne alighted from the wagon and moved up the steps to the platform with a remarkably firm step. His spiritual advisers, Rev. Messrs. Kerfoot and A. A. Reese, accompanied him. He was dressed in fatigue uniform, with a small black shawl thrown over his shoulders. On reaching the scaffold an address was made by Mr. Reese, and prayer was offered by Mr. Kerfoot. The rope was adjusted on the neck of Kuhne by the acting provost marshal, who read the finding of the court-martial and the death warrant, when Col. Morris inquired if he had anything to say before death. The doomed man replied that he had not.

In another instant the drop fell with a dull, heavy sound, and Joseph Kuhne was suspended in mid-air. The drop was only about eighteen inches but for a few minutes no motion was observable. After that his contortions were horrible for a minute, after which he hung still and lifeless.

In the fall the knot failed to draw at the proper place, and had the effect to produce strangulation instead of dislocation.

General Dix and staff were present and occupied a position near the gallows until the execution was completed. After hanging thirty minutes the surgeon examined the body and pronounced life extinct, when it was cut down and placed in charge of Mr. John H. Weaver, undertaker, who by request of the friends of the executed man, took it to Mount Carmel Cemetery for interment. This was the first military execution within the department, . . .

Baltimore *Sun*, March 8, 1862

During the spring of 1861 many Marylanders, hoping their state would secede from the Union, expressed their Southern sympathies in newspapers, broadsides, "secession cards," "patriotic" envelopes, songs and sheet music. They bought photographs of Jefferson Davis, wore red-and-white secession badges, and displayed Confederate flags. When federal troops occupied Baltimore in May, 1861, officials acted quickly to suppress all such acts of disloyalty.

Marylanders demonstrated their support for the Union cause by forming Union clubs and ladies' aid societies, flying U.S. flags, using patriotic envelopes, singing songs, and staging concerts and fairs to raise money and supplies for the army. Maryland's division of the U.S. Sanitary Commission—a volunteer "army" of doctors, nurses, and civilians who tended to the medical and spiritual needs of the vast numbers of wounded—was quite active, particularly after the battles of Antietam and Gettysburg. Union ladies held regular "Sanitary Fairs" to raise money for medical supplies, food, and clothing. The Maryland Bible Society and the U.S. Christian Commission cared for the spiritual side of the Union soldier's life.

RECRUITS WANTED

FOR THE TWELFTH

REGIMENT VOLUNTEER INFANTRY!

TO SERVE

100 DAYS!

PAY, RATIONS & CLOTHING

The same as given to Volunteers now in the service.

They will be employed to occupy the works around the city of Baltimore, guard the railroads, and perform such other duties WITHIN THE STATE, as may be assigned to them by the Commanding General of this Military Department, and IN NO CASE REQUIRED TO DO DUTY OUTSIDE THE STATE without their consent.

Should it become necessary at the end of the ten days from this date to make a Draft to complete the number required, such Draft will then be made under the authority of the Act of Assembly aforesaid, and those so drafted will be subject to orders for duty at any point to which they may be assigned.

LOVERS OF YOUR COUNTRY!

NOW IS THE TIME TO SHOW YOUR PATRIOTISM.

The undersigned have full authority from his Excellency, Gov. Bradford, to recruit for said Regiment.

Persons who desire to Enlist in this Noble Cause, can call upon

Capt. GEO. W. SHRIVER or Lieut. W. P. COLE,

Recruiting Officers,

At

May 14th, 1864.

This recruiting broadside appeared late in the war. The 12th Maryland Infantry was one of the last regiments recruited and saw little service. Union Room Committee, Baltimore.

"Waiting in Line of Battle." Wash drawing by William L. Sheppard, 1867. Col. Bradley Johnson rallies the 1st Maryland (C.S.A.) near Boatswain's Creek, Virginia, during the Seven Days' battles of June, 1862.

Brother against Brother

The Civil War has long been called a brothers' war, filled with bitterness and tragedy as families divided, members sometimes to face one another on battlefields from Virginia to Missouri. In July, 1863, Private Wesley Culp returned to his home town of Gettysburg in the dusty gray of the Army of Northern Virginia — to die on the rugged slopes of Culp's Hill, within sight of the farm on which he had been born. Few moments could be more poignant, yet in this war such meetings of time, place, and past were far from uncommon.

Marylanders, of course, divided in almost every conceivable way. The attack on the 6th Massachusetts had more than the military effect of bringing on the occupation of Baltimore and much of Maryland by federal troops. The riot, Northern reaction, and the sight of federal regiments forced Marylanders to make the painful decision they had thus far postponed. Governor Hicks set up no administrative machinery to implement Lincoln's initial call for 75,000 volunteers, and so not one Marylander answered, but Union military companies, some organized in 1860, defiantly resisted the attempts of state authorities to disarm them. Southern companies met, too, but with regiments from New York and Massachusetts moving quickly through the state, it was clear that they could not long remain. Marylanders who supported the Southern Confederacy or who simply could not abide the idea of federal coercion holding the Union together made the wrenching decision to leave home and family and take up arms. In groups or singly, their numbers never to be known, they slipped across the Potomac to join Virginia regiments mobilizing in Richmond. Some went to Harper's Ferry, where a Maryland regiment was taking shape.

Proud young men from Cecil County rest arms to pose for a passing photographer in 1862. Recruited in Elkton by the 5th Maryland regiment, traditionally from Baltimore, Company I fought at "Bloody Lane" during the Battle of Antietam, saw action in the Shenandoah Valley in 1863 and the siege of Petersburg a year later, and was with that part of the Army of the Potomac that occupied Richmond in 1865. In June 1863, the 5th Maryland was among the Union troops trapped at Winchester, Virginia, by the entire Confederate Army of Northern Virginia. Twenty-eight men from Company I, including three officers, were taken prisoner. Maryland State Archives (Robert G. Merrick Collection) MSA SC 1477-5811.

On May 3 Lincoln issued a second call, for 500,000 volunteers to serve for three years. More than 9,000 Marylanders signed up, but the state's quota was 15,500—evidence that Union sentiment in Maryland stopped well short of genuine war fervor. A great many Union men joined regiments pledged only to guard Maryland soil from any Southern invasion, not to invade the South themselves.

Maryland's amiable social fabric was soon ripped into fiery shreds. On the night of April 19, two omnibuses filled with men of the pro-Southern "Maryland Guard" and Towsontown Cavalry arrived in Cockeysville bent on burning the Northern Central Railroad bridge. They asked for "Hayfield" Merryman but met instead Merryman's neighbor, John W. Wilson, a tough

Mexican War veteran who had organized the Union Rifles. Wilson rejected an offer of five hundred dollars and told them they could burn the bridge over his dead body. The armed party returned to Baltimore.[1] Mc-Henry Howard, studying for the bar, headed south, eventually to join the staff of Confederate Gen. Charles S. Winder, while attorney John R. Kenly in May assumed command of the 1st Maryland Infantry (Union). In June Gen. Nathaniel P. Banks, commanding Union troops in Baltimore, appointed Kenly provost-marshal to replace pro-Southern Marshal George P. Kane, whose efforts on behalf of the 6th Massachusetts were not sufficient proof of loyalty. Kane's sons promptly went south. In Westminster the prominent Shriver clan split as pro-Southern sons departed a staunchly Unionist father. Rising young gentleman and baseball star William Murray led his Waverly team to two victories over the Baltimore Excelsiors in 1861, then took his best players and many members of the prestigious Maryland Guard to Harper's Ferry and the 1st Maryland Regiment (Confederate). The Plug Uglies, once rulers of Baltimore's streets with the Blood Tubs and Rip Raps, declared for the Union. Rival gangs likely went south. Reform mayor George William Brown, who had been elected to combat gang violence and who had tried to stop it on April 19, was soon in jail on charges of "disloyalty" along with elderly millionaire Ross Winans, a congressman, and thirty-one members of the legislature.

Maryland's house had divided, but Maryland was not alone. Much the same thing occurred in Kentucky and Missouri, in Tennessee and in Virginia. Men of both sides stood on principle. Some partings were bitter, others friendly and sad. But the men who went to war in 1861 had one thing in common and in that thing they were terribly wrong. All expected the fighting to begin quickly and end decisively, one or two critical battles to settle the issue in a matter of months, much as it had been in the most recent war in American memory, with Mexico. They had no idea what lay ahead.

"Mosby's Boys." The sons of Baltimore Police Marshal Kane went south early in the war, eventually to join John Singleton Mosby's Confederate irregular cavalry. Ross J. Kelbaugh.

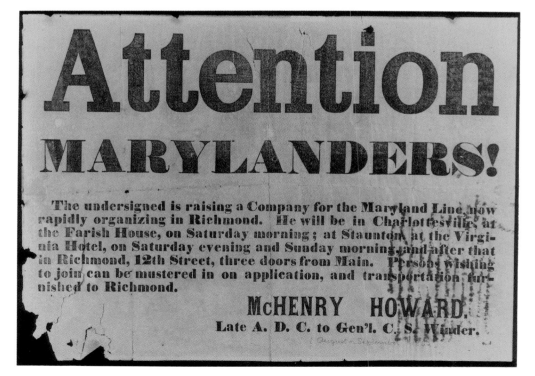

The grandson of James McHenry and John Eager Howard, McHenry Howard served on the staff of Gen. Charles S. Winder with Gen. Thomas J. Jackson's Army of the Valley. In 1862 he recruited Marylanders for the Maryland Line in the Confederate army. The Maryland Line, consisting of all-Maryland units, was the fond dream of many pro-Southern Marylanders, but its organization proved impractical. It existed only briefly in the winter of 1863–64.

Pvt. John Hayden
2d Maryland Infantry, C.S.A.
Courtesy, Frederick D. Shroyer

Pvt. Mark O. Shriver
Union Mills, Carroll County
Co. K, 1st Virginia Cavalry
Courtesy, Historical Society of Carroll County

Pvt. Hamilton Lefevre
Co. L, 1st Virginia Cavalry
Courtesy, Frederick D. Shroyer

Sgt. Thomas Butler
Co. D, 2d Maryland Infantry, C.S.A.
Wounded at Cold Harbor, Virginia, June, 1864
Courtesy, Frederick D. Shroyer

Capt. William H. Murray
Co. A, 2d Maryland Infantry, C.S.A.
Killed at Culp's Hill, Gettysburg, July 3, 1863
Courtesy, Frederick D. Shroyer

Capt. James McHenry Howard
Baltimore City
Staff officer, A.A.G. of the Engineer Corps
Courtesy, Hampton National Historic Site,
National Park Service

Pvt. David Keener Shriver
Union Mills, Carroll County
Enlisted in a Pennsylvania Regiment
Courtesy, Historical Society of Carroll County

Lt. Col. Benjamin F. Taylor
Baltimore City
Staff officer, 2d Maryland Infantry, U.S.

Sgt. Hanson Thomas Murray
Hampstead, Carroll County
Co. I, 6th Maryland Infantry, U.S.
Died of wounds received at Locust Grove,
Virginia, December 19, 1863
Courtesy, Historical Society of Carroll County

Sgt. Alfred L. Benjamin
Kent County
Co. B, 2d Regiment Eastern Shore Infantry, U.S.
Courtesy, Union Room Collection

Lt. Col. Henry Howard, Jr.
Baltimore City
Staff officer, 2d Maryland Infantry, U.S.
Died of wounds received at the Crater,
Petersburg, Virginia, July 21, 1864.

Cpl. John Wolf
Westminster, Carroll County
Co. A, 6th Maryland Infantry, U.S.
Killed at Winchester, Virginia, June 15, 1863
Courtesy, Historical Society of Carroll County

Franklin Buchanan.

McKean Buchanan.

Born in Talbot County, Franklin Buchanan enjoyed a distinguished career in the U.S. Navy, particularly during the Mexican War, before resigning his commission in April, 1861, when he thought his state would join the Confederacy. Soon recruited by Jefferson Davis to lead the Confederate navy, he commanded the attack by the ironclad *Virginia* on U.S. vessels in Hampton Roads.

In a dramatic case of "brother against brother," Buchanan and the *Virginia* (formerly the USS *Merrimac*) on March 8, 1862, attacked and sank the Union blockade ship *Congress*, on which his older brother, McKean, served as paymaster. During the engagement, the *Merrimac* also burned and sank the USS *Cumberland* (pictured below). The crews of both Union ships suffered heavy casualties. McKean Buchanan was not injured during the fight, but Franklin, firing a rifle from the deck of the *Virginia* in the heat of battle, was shot in the thigh and had to be relieved of command a day before the famous battle of the ironclads.

Promoted to admiral in August, Franklin Buchanan commanded naval forces in Mobile Bay, was wounded and captured during the Battle of Mobile Bay in 1864, briefly imprisoned, and exchanged. After the war he served as president of the Maryland Agricultural College (now the University of Maryland) but resigned and took up residence in Mobile. He returned to Talbot County before his death in 1874 and is buried at Wye House. He is here pictured late in the war.

McKean Buchanan lost his life in the naval engagement at Bayou Tech, Louisiana, in January, 1863.

CSS Virginia *attacking USS* Congress *and USS* Cumberland *off Hampton Roads, March 8, 1862. The next day, when the* Virginia *steamed out to attack the USS* Minnesota, *it found instead the first Union ironclad, the USS* Monitor. *The ensuing fight was a standoff, but the* Virginia *was later burned to avoid capture.*

Bradley T. Johnson. Historical
Society of Frederick County.

Front Royal

"Go it, boys!
Maryland whip Maryland!"

John R. Kenly

In May, 1862, in an effort to keep Union armies in the Shenandoah Valley at bay and prevent further reinforcements to the Army of the Potomac, then nearly upon Richmond, Robert E. Lee dispatched Thomas J. "Stonewall" Jackson on his famous Valley Campaign. By driving his men fiercely, Jackson brilliantly outmaneuvered Union forces led by Gen. Nathaniel P. Banks, erstwhile military commander of Baltimore, now encamped at Strasburg. In Banks's command was Col. John R. Kenly's 1st Maryland Volunteer Infantry, stationed at Front Royal on the Manassas railroad to guard against guerrilla raids. Neither garrison suspected Jackson's advance.

With Jackson was the Confederate 1st Maryland. Caught up in the enthusiasm as Jackson's hard-marching outfits swung north down the Valley Pike, they strode along at a seventeen-mile-a-day pace singing:

Baltimore, ain't you happy,
We'll anchor by and by.
We'll stand the storm, it won't be long,
We'll anchor by and by.

On May 22 Jackson halted ten miles from Front Royal and its unprepared garrison. Before first light they were on the march, and by early afternoon they had neared the small town. Learning that it was occupied by the Union 1st Maryland, Jackson halted his column to let the Maryland Confederates pass to the front. Eagerly they formed line of battle with a battalion of "Louisiana Tigers."

About two o'clock in the afternoon they swept down from the hills into Front Royal and chased the surprised federals through the town. As they rushed through the streets, a girl of about fifteen ran out of her house waving a Confederate flag and shouting, "Go it, boys! Maryland whip Maryland!"

On the outskirts north of town the cheering Confederate Marylanders met Kenly's hastily drawn up 1st Maryland. Thinking he was fighting a small guerrilla force, not one that outnumbered him seventeen-to-one, Kenly rallied his men, but in the face of larger numbers soon withdrew across the Shenandoah River to keep from being cut off by encircling Confederate cavalry. Jackson, intent on killing or capturing every federal, sent for his guns and ordered repeated cavalry charges. Kenly fell back from one position to the next, fighting determinedly for several hours until almost completely surrounded. Some of his regiment then broke ranks to flee and were captured by the cavalry. Others, according to a Confederate present, when pursued by the cavalry would "form in small squares and fight to the death."[2] Superior numbers prevailed, and when it was over 904 of Kenly's 1,063 men had been killed or captured. That night the Maryland "rebels" stood guard over the Maryland "loyals" and in the morning jubilantly brought them back into Front Royal. Though newspapers reported that the prisoners received harsh treatment from the Confederate Marylanders, Kenly adamantly denied it and claimed that he and his men were treated with kindness and courtesy.

Left: Maj. Gen. Arnold Elzey, from Somerset County, was a West Pointer, a veteran of the Mexican War, and at the fall of Fort Sumter had command of the U.S. arsenal at Augusta, Georgia. He escorted his troops home to Washington, then resigned from the army to become colonel of the 1st Maryland Infantry, C.S.A. in June, 1861. After service at Manassas, Elzey was promoted to brigadier general and later commanded a brigade under Stonewall Jackson throughout the Valley Campaign. After 1862, as a major general, Elzey assumed command of Richmond's defenses.

Right: George Hume "Maryland" Steuart, the son of Gen. George Hume Steuart, commander of the Maryland militia in the Mexican War period, was also a West Point graduate and served on the western frontier. After the Pratt Street riot he resigned from the army and was commissioned a captain of cavalry in the Confederacy. Upon the formation of the 1st Maryland Infantry, C.S.A., Steuart was appointed lieutenant colonel; less than a year later, at age thirty-three, he was promoted to brigadier general and placed in command of a brigade in Ewell's Division. Along with members of the 2d Maryland Infantry, he distinguished himself at Culp's Hill during the Battle of Gettysburg. In the late spring of 1864 Steuart was captured, held for a few months, then exchanged.

CAMP OF THE MASSACHUSETTS SECOND COMP'Y, LIGHT ARTILLERY
AT STEWARTS PLACE, BALTIMORE, M?

During the federal occupation of Baltimore in 1861, federal officials seized General Steuart's country house on West Baltimore Street for use as a military hospital. This contemporary print shows the barracks, tents, and hospital of the compound. The local lithography firm of E. Sachse & Co. printed this view and others like it of other federal military sites around Baltimore for sale to Union soldiers stationed there as a memento or to send home to family and friends. This one is entitled "Camp of the Massachusetts Second Company, Light Artillery at Stewarts Place, Baltimore, Md."

Lloyd Tilghman, scion of Maryland's prominent Eastern Shore family, attended West Point and later worked as an engineer for the Baltimore and Susquehanna and Baltimore & Ohio railroads. At the commencement of the war he was working as an engineer on the Isthmus of Panama and quickly offered his services to the Confederacy. He was soon appointed brigadier general and served in the western campaigns. Tilghman was captured in Kentucky in 1862 and exchanged, only to meet his death by an exploding shell in Mississippi in May, 1863.

Isaac Ridgway Trimble, a West Point graduate and chief engineer for the Baltimore and Susquehanna Railroad, had been commissioned by Mayor George William Brown to take command of volunteers in the city after the Pratt Street riot. There was little doubt in anyone's mind that his "Volunteer Un-Uniformed Corps" was composed of mainly Southern sympathizers. In May, at age fifty-nine, Trimble crossed the Potomac and was soon commissioned a brigadier general in the Confederate army, commanding the Fourth Brigade, Second Division, supporting Stonewall Jackson in the Valley Campaign of 1862. He distinguished himself at Cross Keys, Richmond, Cold Harbor, and Second Manassas and was promoted to major general. At Gettysburg, he led his division during Pickett's charge, was severely wounded (losing his right leg), captured, and held prisoner until April, 1865.

Raphael Semmes, of Charles County, commanded a ship for the U.S. Navy in the Mexican War but resigned from government service in February, 1861. In April he took command of the Confederacy's first warship and during the next six months captured seventeen U.S. merchant ships. In June, 1862, Captain Semmes assumed command of CSS Alabama. *Over the next twenty-two months, while continuously at sea, Semmes and the* Alabama *captured, ransomed, sank, or burned eighty-two U.S. vessels, gaining widespread fame and notoriety. The Alabama's raids were finally stopped by the USS* Kearsarge *off the coast of Cherbourg when the vessel was sunk and Semmes taken prisoner in June, 1864. The wreck site has been excavated in recent years by French underwater archaeological teams, and recovered artifacts are on exhibit at the Washington Navy Yard. After exchange, Rear Admiral Raphael Semmes took command of the James River Squadron in February, 1865.*

"Charge of the First Maryland Regiment at the Death of Ashby." Lithograph by A. Hoen & Co., Baltimore, 1867, after a painting by W. L. Sheppard.

The Romantic War

In the spring and summer of 1862, at a time when the war brimmed with romantic appeal, the Confederate 1st Maryland regiment was part of Gen. Thomas J. "Stonewall" Jackson's Army of the Valley and a vital participant in that leader's famed Valley Campaign. Marching his men seventeen miles a day on average — some brigades as many as thirty-five — until they earned the nickname "foot cavalry," Jackson confused and defeated three Union armies until, at the battle of Winchester, he drove Gen. Nathaniel P. Banks across the Potomac and had cleared the Shenandoah of federal forces — for about a week. Lincoln, seeing an opportunity to "bag" Jackson, ordered a convergence of Union armies eighty miles behind the Confederate, while Banks, regrouped and reinforced, recrossed the Potomac and headed south, up the Valley Pike in pursuit. Jackson narrowly squeezed through the tightening Union pincers, raced up the pike to Har-

risonburg, and occupied strong ridge positions at Cross Keys and Port Republic.

At Harrisonburg Turner Ashby, one of Jackson's cavalry commanders, a handsome man cut from the cavalier mold and possessed of reckless courage, led several rearguard regiments, including the 1st Maryland, in a brief skirmish against the fast-closing Union army of John C. Fremont. As the fatal minié ball struck him, Ashby is reputed to have urged the Marylanders forward.

The Confederates eventually withdrew to the main army on the ridges above Cross Keys and with two volleys easily repulsed Fremont's assault on their position. The Valley Campaign had ended brilliantly. The ambitious Jackson had secured his place in history, the gallant Ashby a place in the hearts of Virginians. No one, especially those who fought against them, ever forgot the "foot cavalry," either.

The Warrior

Born in 1830 to a family whose men had fought in the Revolutionary, Seminole, and Mexican wars, Richard Snowden Andrews grew up in Washington, D.C., and moved to Baltimore when he was fourteen. His father apprenticed him to a carpenter that he might learn about tools. Apparently the interest took hold because he studied architecture and, believing that war was coming, artillery.

After the riot of April 19, Andrews quickly assumed a military bearing and led a party of five men as far as Bush River to burn railroad bridges into the city. As they were returning, the party captured eighteen "refugees" from the Baltimore fighting and turned them over to a troop of cavalry from Bel Air for imprisonment, although not before making the Unionists swear—lacking a Bible, the oath was made upon a huge Latin Dictionary—never again to invade Maryland soil. Ready to punish the federal officer who had trained his guns on Baltimore, Andrews joined a body of men marching on Fort McHenry, but, when the attack was never made, formed plans to organize his own battery of artillery. From the Pikesville armory he removed inspection reports for twelve-pound Napoleons tested in Massachusetts and arranged to have similar guns cast from his own drawings at a Baltimore forge. He then went to Frederick, where the assembly was meeting, to ask for an appropriation. The legislature refused to contemplate such a thing, and Andrews sped to Harper's Ferry and from there to Richmond, where Governor Letcher immediately commissioned him and let him cast guns for his battery at the Tredegar Iron Works.

Andrews's 1st Maryland Artillery joined the Army of Northern Virginia after the first battle of Bull Run, participated in the Seven Days' battles the following spring, and was with Stonewall Jackson's columns in the Shenandoah in August. It was there, at the Battle of Cedar Run on August 9, 1862, that Andrews sustained the wound that would make him a legend in the army and in Maryland. Galloping toward his guns, which had opened fire on Union forces, he was struck in the lower right side by a shell that burned his chest and opened a ten-inch gash in his abdominal wall.

Richard Snowden Andrews. Courtesy, Frederick D. Shroyer.

Andrews lowered himself gently to the ground, but his intestines fell through his hands and onto the road. He asked passing Confederate columns for a surgeon, but for hours none came. Finally A. P. Hill recognized him and sent his surgeon, who bound up the wound and had Andrews taken to a farmhouse two miles away.

That Andrews asked not to be taken to a field hospital probably saved his life. After assuring Andrews that he would die, the surgeon picked bits of cloth and grit from the wound, reinserted the intestine, and sewed the wound closed with a rusty needle. A prisoner quickly paroled, Andrews asked to send word to his wife in Baltimore, who arrived with her eight-month-old infant a few weeks later. Andrews's only treatment was to place a cloth wrung out with cold water on the wound. Miraculously he did not contract serious infection and fever. Union forces withdrew toward Manassas and the Second Battle of Bull Run, whose guns the wounded man could hear from his bed. After six weeks Andrews regained his feet and the following spring rejoined the army, although it would be more than a year before he could stand fully erect. For the rest of his life he wore a metal plate sewn to his abdominal cavity.

Sergeant Charles Kettlewell of Howard County poses (seated, far right) with his messmates from Mess No. 3, 1st Maryland Cavalry, C.S.A. in this very rare group image of Confederate soldiers. Originally seven young men had joined together to share rations and cooking duties, but by the time this photograph was taken, one had already been killed in fighting in Maryland. *Maryland State Archives (United Daughters of the Confederacy, Mrs. John H. Hopkins Collection) MSA SC 2106.*

A dashing hero of the Confederacy, John Singleton Mosby (standing, second from left) organized an independent cavalry unit in late 1862 which he operated with daring until the end of the war. After each raid his force would scatter to meet again at a designated time and place. A sizable number of Maryland men served in the unit, as seen here, including the sons of former Baltimore police marshal George P. Kane.

"Camp Scenes taken at Alexandria, Virginia, April 1865." After the fighting had ended, Col. Benjamin F. Taylor of Baltimore assembled the staff and field officers of his 2d Maryland (U.S.) to pose for souvenir photographs. The unit was awaiting the Grand Review of the Army of the Potomac, to be held in Washington on May 22, at which time the entire army would parade past President Andrew Johnson and Generals Grant and Sherman. A week later the men took the trains for Baltimore and officially ended their military careers.

Invasion . . .

This woodcut, from a sketch by F. H. Schell, depicts the effects of war on the residents of Sharpsburg during the Battle of Antietam. As women and children huddle in the basement of a large house, a shell bursts at the window. From The Soldier in Our Civil War: A Pictorial History of the Conflict, 1861–1865 *(New York, 1887).*

or
Deliverance?

"The Rebel Army Crossing the Fords of the Potomac for the Invasion of Maryland," Harper's Weekly, *September 27, 1862.*

The present seems to be the most propitious time since the commencement of the war for the Confederate Army to enter Maryland," Gen. Robert E. Lee wrote to Jefferson Davis on September 3, 1862. And well he might think so. On June 1, with the Army of the Potomac's vast numbers at the gates of Richmond, Lee had taken field command of the Army of Northern Virginia and driven the federals back on their heels, in the process providing the impetus by which Lincoln removed Gen. George B. McClellan from command. At the end of August, Lee had outwitted McClellan's successor, John Pope, and shattered his Army of Virginia at Second Bull Run. By early September, Union military leadership was quarreling with itself and with the administration. In the ranks, frustrated soldiers cursed everyone from Lincoln on down.

Lee apparently decided on a northern invasion as a matter of deduction. He could not stay where he was,

on the battlefield near Manassas, but he was unwilling to try the strengthened defenses around Washington or to retreat toward Richmond. While he could take his army into the Shenandoah Valley for rest and food, that would abandon northern Virginia farms to prowling Union foragers. Lee decided instead to carry the war into the North. He hoped to find recruits for his army in Maryland, rest and feed his troops in the rich farmland, and threaten Pennsylvania. Most importantly, Lee intended to draw the Union armies out of Washington where his corps commanders, James Longstreet and Stonewall Jackson, could use their speed and skill to ultimate advantage. The stakes in any battle Lee invited were high. Across the Atlantic, Great Britain and France were contemplating official recognition of the Confederacy. Another spectacular Southern victory might secure that recognition.

Lee marched his army to Leesburg, where cheering

A Frederick native, Princeton graduate, and lawyer, Bradley Johnson early cast his lot with the Confederacy, recruiting soldiers for the 1st Maryland Infantry, C.S.A. from Richmond in May and June, 1861. When Lee's Army of Northern Virginia invaded Maryland in the summer of 1862, Johnson was made provost-marshal of Frederick and circulated his own handbills urging oppressed Marylanders to join the Confederate army. Later in the war he commanded the cavalry units that raided Baltimore and Carroll counties, taking livestock and burning Gov. Augustus Bradford's home near Baltimore. Courtesy, Warren Rifles Confederate Museum.

TO THE PEOPLE OF MARYLAND!

After sixteen months of oppression more galling than the Austrian tyranny, the Victorious Army of the South brings freedom to your doors. Its standard now waves from the Potomac to Mason and Dixon's Line. The men of Maryland, who during the last long months, have been crushed under the heel of this terrible despotism now have the opportunity for working out their own redemption for which they have so long waited and suffered and hoped.

The Government of the Confederate States is pledged by the unanimous vote of its Congress, by the distinct declaration of its President, the Soldier and Statesman Davis, never to cease this War until Maryland has the opportunity to decide for herself her own fate, untrammeled and free from Federal Bayonets.

The People of the South with unanimity unparalleled have given their hearts to our native State and hundreds of thousands of her sons have sworn with arms in their hands that you shall be free.

You must now do your part. We have the arms here for you.--I am authorized immediately to muster in for the War, Companies and Regiments. The Companies of one hundred men each.--The Regiments of ten Companies. Come all who wish to strike for their liberties and their homes.--Let each man provide himself with a stout pair of Shoes, a good Blanket and a Tin Cup---Jackson's men have no Baggage.

Officers are in Frederick to receive Recruits, and all Companies formed will be armed as soon as mustered in. RISE AT ONCE!

Remember the cells of Fort McHenry! Remember the dungeons of Fort Lafayette and Fort Warren; the insults to your wives and daughters, the arrests, the midnight searches of your houses!

Remember these your wrongs, and rise at once in arms and strike for Liberty and right.

BRADLEY T. JOHNSON,

September 8, 1862.   Colonel C. S. A.

As Confederate columns converged on Sharpsburg in September, 1862, Johnson circulated this broadside urging Marylanders to seize the occasion and join the Army of Northern Virginia. Few recruits appeared.

townspeople brought out buckets of cold water for the parched soldiers and stood on the curbstones to hand them freshly baked pies and bread. On the fourth he began crossing the Potomac. A warm autumn sun sparkled on the water. Columns of dusty, ragged troops waded in gratefully, while here and there a regimental band played "Maryland, My Maryland." A quartermaster profoundly cursed a stalled and tangled team of mules, explaining, "There's only one language that will make mules understand on a hot day that they must get out of the water." Astride his horse in the stream nearby, the pious and normally stern Stonewall Jackson tipped his hat and mildly replied, "Thank you, Major."[1] Lee, who had broken a bone in one hand and badly sprained the other in an incident with his horse, Traveller, crossed in an ambulance.

The dirtiest men I ever saw . . . a most ragged, lean, and hungry set of wolves.

Leighton Parks, of Frederick, quoted in *Century Magazine*, 1905.

Confederate infantry, probably Longstreet's corps, approaching the square at Market Street in Frederick on the morning of September 10, 1862. They are marching west, out of the city, on their way to assault and capture Harper's Ferry. Historical Society of Frederick County.

On September 6 the first Confederates reached Frederick, where they found a much different welcome than in Leesburg. "A dirtier, filthier, more unsavory set of human beings never *strolled* through a town," scowled Dr. Lewis H. Steiner. "Faces looked as if they had not been acquainted with water for weeks: hair, shaggy and unkempt. A motlier group was never herded together. But *these* were the chivalry — the deliverers of Maryland from Lincoln's oppressive yoke." Most Frederick residents seemed to agree. Southern sympathizers cheered and brought out water for the soldiers; other citizens defiantly waved Union flags. Most simply glared suspi-

ciously. Only a handful of the young men eyeing the tattered columns joined up.[2]

In Washington, Lincoln reluctantly returned command of the Army of the Potomac to McClellan, or as the cheering soldiers fondly called him, "Little Mac." McClellan reorganized the army's command and with great fanfare — because he regarded himself as the nation's savior and only competent military mind — put 85,000 men on the road to Western Maryland to find Lee. Convinced that Lee had crossed the Potomac with 120,000 men (the actual number was fewer than 40,000), McClellan moved with his customary caution.

General McClellan with his staff rode through, and was received on all sides with the most unlimited expressions of delight . . . matrons held their babes towards him as their deliverer from the rule of a foreign army, and fair young ladies rushed to meet him on the streets, some even throwing their arms around his horse's neck.

Dr. Lewis H. Steiner, September 13, 1862

"General McClellan Entering the Town of Frederick, Maryland — The Popular Welcome," Harper's Weekly, *October 4, 1862.*

The correspondent for Harper's *reported that "flags were displayed upon all the houses" and the town was "overjoyed" as Gen. George B. McClellan arrived in Frederick. Out of favor with Lincoln, "Little Mac" was nevertheless a favorite with the hard-fighting Army of the Potomac — and with the cheering crowd. Announcing that he had "driven the rebels from the place," he moved on and defeated Lee's rear guard on September 14 at South Mountain — the first major engagement on Maryland soil. Three days later the armies would meet again.*

Taking advantage of the federals' slow pace, Confederate cavalry commander J. E. B. Stuart organized a grand ball at the female academy in Urbana, southeast of Frederick, to which all the young ladies of the region were invited. Rested and bathed, their uniforms brushed, his officers danced in splendid cavalier fashion while the 18th Mississippi's regimental band played through the night.

Before Lee could deal with McClellan or move north into Pennsylvania, one detail remained. The federal garrisons at Martinsburg and Harper's Ferry, 13,000 men in all, had not followed conventional military wisdom and retreated as Lee advanced. He decided to sweep them up, and on September 9 wrote out orders that would split his army into four columns — three would march on Harper's Ferry from different directions; the fourth would hold the passes through imposing South Mountain until all could reunite. At 4 A.M. on September 10th, in high spirits and marching to "The Girl I Left Behind Me," the Army of Northern Virginia swung west out of Frederick.

A full two days later, lead elements of the Army of the Potomac raced into the town. While townspeople took cover and anxiously listened, a rear-guard detachment of Wade Hampton's cavalry won a small battle in the streets, then trotted confidently out one side of town as Union infantry rushed in from the

Right and below: These rarely seen photographs of the well-supplied Army of the Potomac marching through Frederick in pursuit of Lee's army, either in September, 1862, or July, 1864, may have been taken by the same photographer who captured the ragged Confederates. B'nai B'rith International, Washington, D.C.

"Hagerstown, Maryland, While Occupied by the Rebels." Harper's Weekly, *September 27, 1862.*

other. On September 13, a Saturday, McClellan himself rode into Frederick on his majestic black horse, Dan Webster, to the population's evident relief.

The cheers that greeted him were nothing compared to the military riches that were about to befall McClellan. In a meadow outside Frederick two men from the 27th Indiana found three cigars wrapped in an official-looking document that turned out to be Lee's Order No. 191, detailing the routes and schedules Lee's separated columns had taken. On receiving it, McClellan turned from an adoring delegation of townspeople and literally whooped with joy, shouting, "Now I know what to do!" Though he continued to overestimate Lee's numbers, he did know where the Confederate army was and that it was dangerously divided, with sixty miles between Jackson and Longstreet. McClellan, who was also known (not always respectfully) as "the Young Napoleon," vowed that the defeat he was

about to inflict on Lee would overshadow the exploits of his namesake.[3]

Had McClellan begun promptly he might have crushed Lee's columns piecemeal and ended the war. Lee had even aided him by sending some of his remaining troops to Hagerstown, leaving only five thousand men to hold Turner's and Fox's Gaps, the two major breaches in the mountain. Had the Army of the Potomac pushed aside this tiny force and entered the valley beyond, it would have found itself between Jackson and Longstreet with twice their combined strength.

Yet McClellan dallied. Eighteen hours passed between the time he received the lost order and when the first regiments marched, and then the pace was slow. When at last the federals reached South Mountain on September 14, McClellan believed Lee to be waiting with the bulk of his army just on the other side. Despite his perpetual belief that he was facing superior num-

"Battle of South Mountain, Md. Sept. 14, 1862. General Hatch's Brigade driving the Rebels over the top of the Mountain toward Sharpsburg."

bers, he assaulted Turner's Gap with a single brigade. A sharp fight followed, as McClellan sent in more troops against the outmanned Confederates, who managed to hold the passes just long enough for reinforcements to arrive from Hagerstown and Harper's Ferry. Lee fell back to the high ground west of Antietam Creek, near the small town of Sharpsburg, and coolly awaited the return of his far-flung columns.

Though McClellan outnumbered Lee, even by his own exaggerated estimates of Lee's strength, he did not attack the Confederate line on September 15. The following day was foggy, and though he had personally ridden close enough to the Confederate line — a mile and one-half long stretching across the ridge west of the Antietam — to invite rebel cannon fire, the Union general delayed one more day as more of his troops came up. Unfortunately for the Army of the Potomac, Harper's Ferry surrendered on the fifteenth. Union soldiers heard the Confederates cheering as word reached their lines and realized that while "Little Mac" had delayed, the bulk of the Confederate army was now on the road to Sharpsburg.

"Looking North — Morning, Antietam Battlefield," by Capt. James Hope, from sketches made at the scene. Captain Hope, of the 2d Vermont Infantry, gave this rendering of Col. Stephen D. Lee's Confederate artillery, Jackson corps, firing into Gen. John Sedgwick's Union battle lines attacking from the East Woods. The cornfield, already in Union hands, is at far center, the Dunker Church at upper left. Antietam National Battlefield, National Park Service/Larry Sherer.

Antietam

When I took that color in my hand, I gave up all hope of life.

Maj. Rufus Dawes, 6th Wisconsin Infantry

Dawn on September 17, 1862, was ominously dark. A light drizzle dampened cook fires and rifle barrels as Union troops deployed in line of battle. McClellan's right wing was to begin the attack by moving southward down both sides of the Hagerstown Pike toward a plateau west of Antietam Creek marked by a small white church. Shortly thereafter, McClellan's left wing was to cross a sturdy stone bridge nearly a mile to the south of the church and force the Confederate right wing back toward Sharpsburg. After he had turned both Confederate flanks, McClellan would launch his reserves at the Confederate center and sweep the field.

When the order came, men from Massachusetts, Wisconsin, Pennsylvania, Michigan, and New Jersey stepped off from a line of trees, now called the North Woods, across rolling farm land on either side of the pike. Stonewall Jackson had arrived a day earlier, and his guns near the church and on high ground west of the pike opened fire with solid shot that screamed close overhead, bounced wildly over the ranks, or tore sudden, bloody gaps in their midst. Behind them federal cannon opened a devastating counter-battery fire. The Union battle line crossed a fallow field and entered one of standing corn between two more wooded areas, the East and West Woods.

Awaiting them behind a sturdy fence on the other side of a small clover field just beyond the corn was Stonewall Jackson's entire corps. Though they took a heavy beating from Union artillery they could not see, Jackson's veterans held their fire until the Union line emerged into the open, then shattered it with their first volleys. Rebel counterattacks drove the federals back across the cornfield until they, too, were cut down in a

Each canister contains several hundred balls. They fell in the very front of the line and all along it apparently, stirring up a dust like a thick cloud. When the dust blew away no regiment and not a living man was to be seen.

Gen. Alpheus Williams, September 22, 1862

Confederate dead on the ridge just south of the cornfield, a position from which Stonewall Jackson's artillery raked Union battle lines. Stereo view by Alexander Gardner, September 19, 1862. Library of Congress/Ross J. Kelbaugh.

The crying of the wounded for water, the shrieks of the dying, mingled with the screeching of the shells, made up a scene so truly appalling and horrible that I hoped to God, that I might never witness such another.

James H. Rigby, Battery A, 1st Maryland Light Artillery, September 19, 1862

*"View in the Field, on the west side of Hagerstown road, after the Battle of Antietam."
Stereo view by Alexander Gardner, September 19, 1862. Library of Congress.
Looking north along the Hagerstown Pike. These troops were probably Louisianians, part
of Stonewall Jackson's reserve. Jackson's first line held its ground against a federal battle
line advancing down the pike for forty-five minutes until forced to fall back. Two reserve
brigades advanced from the West Woods (to the rear of the camera position) and wheeled
to their right to meet federal pressure from the cornfield on the far side of the double fence
bordering the pike.*[2]

A tremendous battle has been going on today from daylight till dark near Sharpsburg, Keedysville, and Bakersville. The cannons and musketry have been roaring all day. . . . I rode on to the battle field where the Rebels formed their line of battle. They were not buried. I could see their line distinctly by the dead lying along it as they fell. Nearly all lying on their backs as if they hadn't even made a struggle. The line I suppose was a mile long or more.

Otho Nesbitt,
Clear Spring Maryland,
September 17, 1862

vicious fire. For four hours the armies advanced and retreated through the small cornfield. Losses on both sides were staggering. The 12th Massachusetts took 334 men into the cornfield; 112 came out. Advancing federal artillery had to unpile the bodies before they could open fire. A young correspondent went to the cornfield late in the morning and saw what looked like an entire Confederate regiment lying in formation, their weapons and accoutrements thrown in every direction. So much blood spilled onto the shattered cornstalks and into the ground that men grew sick at the sight and smell.

By late morning Union troops, including the 3rd Maryland and the small Purnell Legion, succeeded in driving Confederate guns off the plateau near the Dunker Church and advanced half a mile into the West Woods just beyond it. There, a surprise Confederate counterattack caught them in a murderous crossfire. In a panic they fled back across the cornfield — it would forever after be known as *the Cornfield* — into the safety of the East Woods, surrendering nearly all their hard-won ground.

"Looking South — Afternoon, Antietam Battlefield," by Capt. James Hope from sketches made at the scene. In this Hope painting, the 7th Maine Infantry crosses the ghastly sunken road or "bloody lane" in pursuit of retreating Confederates and advances toward Rebel artillery and infantry rallying in the distance. The assault of the 7th Maine proved futile — two-thirds were cut down within twenty minutes. Antietam National Battlefield, National Park Service/Larry Sherer.

Late in the morning, several Union brigades attacking westward toward the church wandered a little to their left, toward the undefended Confederate center. Lee rushed two regiments of Alabamians and North Carolinians into a rutted and deeply eroded country lane protected from Union artillery by slightly higher ground to its front. Frantically the rebels pulled down fence rails from one side of the lane and piled them in their front on the other to make a crude but effective breastwork that Col. John B. Gordon of the 6th Alabama promised to hold "until the sun goes down."

For a time, it seemed he would keep his word. The first Union regiments to march over the hill, including the 5th Maryland, were shattered by a withering fire that sent them retreating to the safety of the lee slope. With their green battle flags unfurled, the Irish Brigade — composed of Irishmen recruited from New York City — proudly advanced in line of battle to the ridge above the lane to renew the assault. Half their lead regiment, the 63rd New York, went down in the first Confederate volley. The Irishmen stood their ground, trading fire with an enemy not seventy-five yards away — point blank range for Civil War rifles. As they fell in horrifying numbers, their officers pleaded with troops concealed on the sheltered side of the slope to come to their

support, but only a handful did. Finally, decimated and out of ammunition, what was left of the brigade with defiant precision formed into a column of fours, wheeled, and slowly marched to safety. More Union regiments came up.

In the road, all was chaos. Confederate reinforcements piled in until men could hardly move and those in the rear had to pass loaded rifles to the front. Eventually Union troops found a bluff high above and on the north side of the lane, from which they could fire down its length. Once nearly impregnable, the lane in moments became a deadly enclosure. Colonel Gordon of the 6th Alabama was hit twice in the right calf, in the upper left arm, then in his left shoulder. He staggered down the line, encouraging his men, until he came to a dying Joseph Johnson, lying protectively beside the body of a younger man. "Here we are," Johnson told his colonel. "My son is dead, and I shall go soon, but it is all right."[1] A sixth ball hit Gordon in the face, and he pitched forward into his hat. Only a bullet hole that let the blood escape saved him from drowning. Confederate casualties mounted swiftly, but true to Gordon's word his men held until a misunderstood order resulted in a general retreat and allowed Union troops to finally take the "bloody lane."

Here we are. My son is dead, and I shall go soon, but it is all right.

Pvt. Joseph A. Johnson, 6th Alabama Infantry, in the Sunken Road, September 17, 1862

"Confederate dead in Bloody Lane." Stereo view by Alexander Gardner, September 19, 1862, showing the carnage in "Bloody Lane," where a Union officer counted the bodies of five hundred Confederates in the space of two hundred feet. Burial parties had been at work for some time when Gardner took this photograph, and much of the lane had been cleared. The group of corpses in the foreground suggests how much of the lane looked before the burials and is indicative of the courageous fight these men waged for two and one-half hours, and their fate once federal troops breached their lines and fired down the length of the lane. The men were from North Carolina. Library of Congress.

The battle for Burnside's Bridge is shown in this detail from "Looking West, Noon to Three P.M." Painting by Capt. James Hope, from sketches made at the scene. Antietam National Battlefield, National Park Service/Larry Sherer.

Despite its terrible losses in the Cornfield and the Sunken Road, the Army of the Potomac might have overwhelmed Lee with its superior numbers had McClellan's plan to attack the bridge on the Confederate right flank been carried out on time. But while fighting raged elsewhere, Gen. Ambrose Burnside's Ninth Corps delayed its attack, even as Lee stripped defenses in that area until only four hundred men of the 2d Georgia remained. When the first Union attacks did come, they were half-hearted attempts that the Georgians easily repulsed. At Burnside's headquarters, staff and regimental officers quarreled; it seemed impossible to mount anything like a concerted push on the bridge. Several more desultory assaults followed, including an advance led by the 2d Maryland, which lost nearly half its men in a matter of minutes.

Burnside finally managed to capture the bridge as the result of a fluke. With the Georgians running low on ammunition, a Union brigade commander ordered the 51st Pennsylvania to advance. The men were surly, having recently lost their whiskey ration, and greeted the order with contemptuous disobedience. Only when they had extracted a promise that their whiskey ration would be restored did they make the charge in concert with the 51st New York. They carried the bridge — hours too late and only after fighting had ended in the northern portion of the field and was nearing its end in the center. Had Burnside acted quickly he nevertheless might have turned the flank as planned, for Lee's line was by then threadbare, but he delayed again. When he moved, he succeeded in driving the rebels back almost to Sharpsburg only to be stopped by the last-minute arrival of Southern reinforcements who had since morning raced seventeen miles to the battlefield.

The Battle of Antietam, the bloodiest one-day battle in the Civil War, ended in stalemate.

Interior of the Evangelical Lutheran Church, Frederick, Md., September, 1862. Soldiers' cots rest on wooden planking laid across the pews. After the battle, the number of wounded far exceeded the population of tiny Sharpsburg. Churches and public buildings in Williamsport, Keedysville, Boonsboro, Hagerstown, and Frederick served as makeshift hospitals — as did barns for miles about. On the northern edge of the battlefield Union surgeons built a tent city to shelter casualties from both armies. The tents remained as late as December. Evangelical Lutheran Church.

The Civil War was the first major conflict in our history to be preserved by means of the camera. Developed in France in 1839, photography quickly captured the popular imagination, and by 1860 photograph albums were introduced to house the very popular cartes-de-visite. Soon no parlor was considered complete without an album filled with pictures of family members, friends, and notables of the day.

Alexander Gardner, a young associate of Matthew Brady, was the first photographer to arrive at the Antietam battlefield. Over the next five days he made some seventy photographs, documenting the unbelievable horror of the war.

In late October, 1862, Brady created a sensation by exhibiting Gardner's photographs in his well-known New York gallery. Hushed groups of potential buyers peered down at the small images, using magnifying glasses to make out the features on lifeless faces.

Brady published these photographs as album cards and stereo views, and soon they were available throughout the Union. For the first time, Americans could see the awful image of war.

"A Contrast: Federal buried, Confederate unburied, where they fell, on Battle-field of Antietam." Stereo view by Alexander Gardner, September 19, 1862. This photograph vividly depicts the bitterness of civil war. A federal soldier looks down on the grave of Lt. John A. Clark, 7th Michigan, a twenty-one-year-old native of Monroe, Michigan, and veteran of the Peninsula Campaign who died north of the Dunker Church. His family came to the battlefield, located his grave, and took the remains home for burial. The Confederate, who remains anonymous, probably lies on or near the battlefield.[3] Library of Congress.

With nearly twenty thousand fresh troops in reserve, McClellan still possessed the means to drive the Army of Northern Virginia into the Potomac. But McClellan, fearing that he had met only a portion of Lee's army and warning that his was the only armed force left to save Washington, held back. The armies laid down on their arms for the night, expecting to resume battle the next day. Mercifully, they did not, instead arranging a truce to bury the dead and carry off the wounded. On the nineteenth, Lee quietly retreated across the Potomac. The over-cautious McClellan did not pursue, ensuring that the war, which might have ended at Antietam, would continue.

Nearly four thousand men from both sides died on the field at Antietam; eighteen thousand suffered horrible wounds. In farmhouses and barns they anxiously awaited the surgeon's knife and bone saw, and listened as terrified screams and pitiful cries filled the night. They probably realized that they had lived through the bloodiest single day in American history, though greater numbers were to fall in other battles — over four thousand in two days at Chickamauga, and seven thousand in three days at Gettysburg. But long after the war those who were there would attest that nothing they subsequently experienced was worse than the single day of Antietam.

Alexander Gardner returned to Antietam to record Lincoln's visit and conference — which grew into a confrontation — with McClellan. When the general refused Lincoln's urgings to move quickly after Lee, Lincoln again removed him from command of the army, this time permanently.

As it is, the dead of the battle-field come up to us very rarely, even in dreams. We see the list in the morning paper at breakfast, but dismiss its recollection with the coffee. . . . Mr. Brady has done something to bring home to us the terrible reality and earnestness of war. If he has not brought bodies and laid them in our door-yards and along streets, he has done something very like it.

New York Times, October 20, 1862

"Confederate Soldiers, as they fell, near the Burnside Bridge, at the Battle of Antietam." Stereo view by Alexander Gardner, September 21, 1862. Library of Congress.

"The Emancipation of the Negroes." Engraving from Harper's Weekly, *January, 1863. George Peabody Library of the Johns Hopkins University.*

Freedom

The Confederate withdrawal from Maryland after the battle of Antietam proved to be the "victory" Lincoln needed as the background for announcing the Emancipation Proclamation, and he did so on September 22, 1862. The proclamation freed all slaves held in "territories in rebellion against the United States" and was to take effect on the first of the year.

But emancipation brought Maryland slaves only a glimpse of the promised day of Jubilee. On January 1, 1863, not one Maryland slave was freed. They returned to fields, factories, and shipyards as before. Some had been thrown into prisons and country jails for safe-keep-

ing while their masters fought in the Confederate army, and there, in indescribable filth, they remained.

Yet the character of slavery had begun to change. From its onset, the war had eroded the "peculiar institution" in the state as elsewhere in the South. Union detachments trudging through Maryland lured slaves away to Union army encampments. Though most Northern soldiers shared the prevailing views of the period — they disliked blacks and rejected outright the idea of racial equality — they barely tolerated slavery and slaveholders. Officers at first refused to permit runaways in the camps, but before long that official position

The 4th Regiment U.S. Colored Troops was organized at Baltimore from July to September, 1863, to serve for three years. Company E, pictured above in 1865, was composed largely of men from Frederick and Carroll counties. The regiment trained in Yorktown, Virginia, and saw duty in the spring of 1864 guarding Confederate prisoners at Point Lookout. Later in 1864 the 4th served with Gen. Benjamin Butler's army in an unsuccessful attack upon Fort Fisher, North Carolina, which, when renewed under another general's command, took the fort and with it the city of Wilmington. After the war, the 4th briefly performed garrison duty in the South until mustered out in May, 1866. Of the 131 men in Company E, twenty-three died from wounds received in battle, and thirteen succumbed to disease. Library of Congress/Ross M. Kimmel.

gave way. Maryland slaveowners who ventured onto the neatly tented company streets in search of their runaway property met at best cold sympathy and sometimes open and threatening hostility. Burly infantrymen called them "nigger drivers" and worse. Other slaves, particularly from Montgomery and Prince George's counties, ran away to Washington, where slavery had been abolished in 1862, and disappeared in the alleys and shanties of the free black community there. Attempts to retrieve them ran afoul of unfriendly and uncooperative military authorities.

The final blow to slavery gathered force in the early months of 1863. Union battlefield failures combined with staggering casualty lists after Shiloh, the Seven

O | 9 | **U. S. C. T.**

Adam Pinckett

............, Co. *G*, 9 Reg't U. S. Col'd Inf.

Appears on

Company Descriptive Book

of the organization named above.

DESCRIPTION.

Age *21* years; height *5* feet *4½* inches.

Complexion *Not very black*

Eyes *Black*; hair *Wooly*

Where born *Salisbury, Md.*

Occupation *Farm hand*

ENLISTMENT.

When *Nov. 22*, 186*3*

Where *Salisbury, Somerset*

By whom *Col. Wm. Birney*, term *3* y'rs.

Remarks: *Strong ? rebel*
Adeline Bird
Slave for life
Corporal
Mustered out with
Regt. Nov. 26, 1866.

W. M. Jackson

(383₀)   *Copyist.*

Enlistment record of Adam Pinkett, 9th Regiment U.S.C.T. Pinkett and his three brothers, all slaves on the Eastern Shore, escaped their masters to join the Union army in October and November, 1863. By late summer of 1864 they were serving in the Colored Brigade as part of General Grant's campaign against Richmond where, at Deep Bottom on the James River, they encountered their heaviest fighting of the war. Harold T. Pinkett.

More blacks at first served in the Union navy than in the army, because blacks' long tradition aboard ships had created a greater degree of acceptance in that branch. This U.S. sailor is from Maryland, but his name is unknown. Ross J. Kelbaugh.

Days' battles, Second Bull Run, Antietam, and Fredericksburg had all but stopped the flow of volunteers into what had become the most terrible and costly of American wars. In April, 1862, the Confederacy had resorted to conscription, and in March, 1863, the Union followed suit. But conscription, even when combined with bounties to lure recruits, failed miserably. Men of means paid a $300 "commutation fee" to escape service or hired substitutes to serve in their places. Those enlisting for the bounties offered by various counties frequently "jumped"—deserted—at the first opportunity, often to enlist elsewhere a few weeks later. Out of the hundreds of thousands conscripted for the Union army, only a handful joined its depleted ranks. Moreover, the idea of conscription proved unpopular in the extreme. Here and there a provost-marshal was shot trying to bring in conscripts, and a few days after the Union victory at Gettysburg, New York City erupted in three days of bloody rioting against the draft.

Many hope they will prove cowards and sneaks — others greatly fear it.

New York *Tribune*, May 1863

For two years abolitionists and Radical Republicans had argued that blacks, free and slave, be allowed to serve in the army. Frederick Douglass in 1861 had urged Lincoln to make use of his "strong black arm." But, fearing the reaction in the border slave states, Lincoln had rejected all such advice. Now, with emancipation in place and a real need for manpower, he acceded — with reservations. In May the War Department established a Bureau of Colored Troops and that summer began recruiting. Secretary of War Edwin M. Stanton tapped William Birney, son of noted abolitionist James G. Birney, to recruit a colored regiment in Baltimore. Birney wrote to his long-time friend, Treasury Secretary Salmon P. Chase, that he felt certain of "striking a heavy blow at the 'institution' in this state," and set to work energetically.[1]

Zealous and resourceful, Birney soon put together several companies of free blacks, among them a dozen Hagerstown musicians who constituted a regimental band. Recruiting parties swept through the state, ostensibly in search of free black recruits but often enticing slaves as well — to the fury of their owners and the consternation of President Lincoln and some of his advisors. Birney loaded his band and a detachment of black soldiers aboard a bay steamer and cruised the Chesapeake tributaries. At plantation docks the band played "sweet music," the soldiers demonstrated the manual of arms, and soon much of the planter's able-bodied labor force was sailing downriver. Birney's men could be forceful and cared little whether a planter inclined toward the Union or the Confederacy. Maryland slaveholders were outraged, and Lincoln drafted a memorandum objecting to offensive conduct in recruiting and to taking slaves from loyal owners without their consent. Birney was undaunted. In late October, 1863, Lincoln authorized the payment to owners of up to $300 compensation for slaves enlisted in the army. The order also declared that "all persons enlisted into the military service shall forever thereafter be free." In all, Maryland furnished 8,700 of the army's 186,000 black troops, including the 4th, 7th, 9th, 19th, 30th, and 39th Regiments, U.S.C.T.

White volunteers initially greeted the black troops with a mixture of scorn and war-weary pragmatism. "What's the use to have men from Maine, Vermont and Massachusetts dying down here in these swamps," one white soldier wrote from Louisiana. "You can't replace these men, but if a nigger dies, all you have to do is send out and get another one." An Iowa private told his wife, "You may be astonished to hear me say that the arming of the negroes is just what we want it meets with nearly universal approbation in the army. I dont care if they are 1/2 mile thick in front in every Battel they will stop Bullets as well as white people." The New York *Tribune* was more perceptive. "Loyal whites have generally become willing that they should fight," it opined in May, 1863, "but the great majority have no faith that they will really do so. . . . Many hope they will prove cowards and sneaks — others greatly fear it."[2]

But black infantry units turned skeptics' minds with courage and blood. Maryland outfits especially proved themselves at Fort Fisher and in the exceedingly bloody Wilderness Campaign in the summer of 1864 that ended in the siege of Petersburg, Virginia. At the Battle of the Crater, in the Petersburg lines, the 7th Maryland met with disaster and earned grudging respect. And the first Union soldiers to set foot in Richmond were a detachment of black cavalry.

"Teaching the Negro Recruits the Use of the Minie Rifle." Engraving from Harper's Weekly, *March 14, 1863.*

The colored troops were last to retire, which they did with unwavering firmness and in obedience to orders, not, however, before they gave three cheers, which evinced their dauntless spirit.

Thomas Morris Chester, black correspondent for the Philadelphia *Press*, Dispatch sent August 18, 1864, from the lines around Richmond

The Crater

By June, 1864, Ulysses S. Grant's bloody offensive toward Richmond had cost fifty thousand Union casualties, nearly a third of his army, and worse, had become stalled in the lines around Petersburg, the railroad gate to Richmond. Both sides settled into a deadly attritional war in the trenches.

The armies resorted to stratagems to break the stalemate. Lee sent Jubal Early to menace Washington and weaken Grant's army for an assault. Inside Union lines, a different sort of plan was afoot. The colonel of a regiment of coal miners from the Schuylkill region of Pennsylvania offered to dig a mine from his lines 150 yards to a redoubt protecting a Confederate battery. His corps commander, Ambrose E. Burnside, approved. As the miners made steady progress with improvised tools — they could not get picks from the quartermaster but had to make their own — even the dubious Grant began to feel their enthusiasm. In a month they had defied their bureaucratic superiors and completed a tunnel five feet high, four feet wide at the bottom and two feet at the top, with a perpendicular explosive chamber seventy-five yards long at the end. This they packed with 320 kegs, each twenty-five pounds, of black powder — four tons in all. Twenty feet above them, having heard their digging and fearing what was about to happen, the Rebels were frantically counter-mining to find what was beneath them. A four-day rest after the federal tunnel was completed convinced the Rebels that the federals had abandoned the effort.

To make the attack after the explosion that was to open a gap — no one knew how wide — in the Rebel lines, Burnside picked his Colored Brigade. All the while the miners dug, the brigade rehearsed the difficult assault until each squad, each man, knew his role. But at the last minute, Grant hesitated. Not wanting to be accused of sending black troops to what might well turn out to be a slaughter — "it would then be said, and very properly," he later testified, "that we were shoving those people ahead to get killed because we did not care anything about them" — he moved them to the rear of the four-brigade assault column and replaced them with an untried white brigade of heavy artillerymen.

At 3:30 on the morning of July 27, with four brigades poised and more in reserve for a follow-up assault, and with 144 guns — more than either side had used at Gettysburg — at the ready, a nervous miner lit the fuse, but nothing happened. Two volunteers entered the tunnel, located where it had burned out, re-lit it, and scurried the long 150 yards out just before the spectacular blast. Recalled a stunned Union captain: "A slight tremor of the earth for a second, then the rocking as of an earthquake, and with a tremendous blast which rent the sleeping hills beyond, a vast column of earth and smoke shoots upward to a great height, its dark sides flashing out sparks of fire, hangs poised for a moment in mid-air, and then, hurtling down with a roaring sound, showers of stones, broken timbers and blackened human limbs, subsides — the gloomy pall of

"Charge of the Phalanx." From The Black Phalanx: A History of the Negro Soldiers of the United States *(Hartford, 1889).*

darkening smoke flushing to an angry crimson as it floats away to meet the morning sun."[3]

Everyone nearby fled in panic. A huge unoccupied gap opened in the Confederate lines, but the assault column, watching the debris falling toward them, huddled for cover. When they moved out they discovered no one had removed the defensive obstacles in their path, and they had to squeeze through an improvised opening ten feet wide. When they reached the awesome crater, sixty feet wide, two hundred feet long, and more than twenty feet deep, instead of fanning out on either side, the lead brigade swarmed down into it. Two more brigades followed, and the ingredients for disaster were at hand. Confederate infantry closed in. Rebel artillery began firing canister into the packed mass in the crater. The colored brigade moved up for its assault, circling around the crater as it had practiced, but the Rebels were now ready for them and mowed down fully a third of their number. The survivors, too, retreated into the crater, now so packed with men unable to climb up the loose dirt sides it was impossible for the Confederates to miss. Union gunners did what they could to silence the Rebel artillery, but a disgusted Grant called off the support column and ordered Burnside to extricate his men. This Burnside, hoping for a miracle, hesitated to do, and for more agonizing hours the slaughter continued, until the Confederates ended it with rapid fire marksmanship on the rim and a bayonet charge. Hundreds of federals surrendered. Thousands fled. Four thousand were lost, half of them captured or missing, when the Battle of the Crater had ended.

Broadside, "Oath of Allegiance," 1864. In the election to ratify the Maryland Constitution of 1864, election judges were given the authority to deny the vote to any who refused to take this loyalty oath or who did not answer satisfactorily questions about their past activities. Southern sympathizers were thus eliminated from the ratification process.

OATH
TO BE ADMINISTERED TO EVERY VOTER.

"I do swear (or affirm) that I am a citizen of the United States, that I have never given any aid, countenance or support to those in armed hostility to the United States, that I have never expressed a desire for the triumph of said Enemies over the Arms of the United States, and that I will bear true faith and allegiance to the United States, and support the Constitution and Laws thereof, as the Supreme Law of the land, any Law or Ordinance of any State to the contrary notwithstanding; that I will in all respects demean myself as a Loyal citizen of the United States, and I make this oath (or affirmation) without any reservation or evasion, and believe it to binding on me."

QUESTIONS
For the use of Judges of Election

1. Service in the Rebel Army.

Have you ever served in the rebel army?

2. Aid to those in Armed Rebellion.

Have you ever given aid to those in rebellion?
Have you never given money to those intending to join the rebellion?
Have you never given money to their agents?
Have you never given money, clothing or provisions for the purpose of aiding the emigration of persons from this State to the South?
Have you never sent money, clothing or provisions to persons in the South since the rebellion?

3. Comfort and Encouragement to Rebellion.

Note.—Comfort or encouragement means advocacy, advice in favor of. We aid the rebellion by giving money, clothing and provisions; we give it comfort and encouragement by our words. A man who has advocated the cause of rebellion, who talked in favor of Maryland going with the South, who rejoiced over the victories of the rebel armies, has given comfort and encouragement to the rebellion.

Have you ever given comfort or encouragement to the rebellion?
Have you never in conversation, attempted to justify the course of the States in rebellion?
Have you never expressed a wish for the success of the rebellion or its army?
Have you never in conversation, discouraged the cause of the Federal Government?
Did you rejoice over the downfall of Fort Sumpter?

4. Disloyalty.

Note.—If the Judges are satisfied that a man is disloyal to the United States; it is their duty to refuse his vote, for such a person is not a "legal voter" of the State of Maryland.

Are you a loyal citizen of the United States?
Have you been loyal ever since the beginning of the war?
Have you ever rejoiced over the defeat of the Union army?
Have you ever rejoiced over the success of the rebel army?
When the Union army and the rebel army meet in battle, which do you wish to gain the victory.

Note.—After interrogating the person offering to vote, the Judges may hear other evidence to prove or disprove his statements, and must be governed by the weight of testimony.

ALL HAIL MARYLAND!

The Maryland soldiers have achieved one of the grandest victories of the war. They have lifted 'the despot's heel' from the shore of their Maryland. Their vote has redeemed their State from the curse of Slavery, and anchored it fast and forever to the Union, whose cause, as the old Continental Congress declared, 'is the cause of human nature.' Their victory shows that they, too, understand the meaning of this war. They perceive that it is the armed insurrection of the privileged few against the laboring many. They know that the great slaveholder is the direct rival of the free laborer who lives by his daily wages. They know that while the system lasts permanent peace is impossible, and having learned in the battle-field and the Southern prison that the tender mercies of slavery are cruel, they have, with one master blow, demolished the root of the war in the soil of Maryland. It is indeed 'a glorious victory.' God bless the Maryland citizens at the front and the Maryland citizens at home!

Harper's Weekly, October 29, 1864

By 1864 it was increasingly clear in the Northern states that slavery could not survive the war. In the spring of 1862, Congress had ended slavery in the District of Columbia, and a militia act in 1862 had freed slaves of masters who entered the Confederate army. The Emancipation Proclamation symbolically freed all slaves of Rebel masters on January 1, 1863. In May, the army began recruiting black troops. In Maryland, as in other border states, the pressure on slaveowners grew intense. Newspapers argued that the value of land was greater when worked by free men. Slaves ran off to the District of Columbia or to the army, or, seeing the end in sight, simply worked less. When Lincoln offered loyal slaveowners $300 in compensation for each manumitted bondsman, army recruiting officers found themselves turning away slaves offered by their masters because they refused to work.

The Maryland Constitution of 1851 required the General Assembly to conduct a referendum after each census to see whether voters desired a new constitutional convention. In the state election of October, 1863, with some delegates running as "Emancipationists" and, as proslavery voters charged, the military influencing the outcome, that process was set in motion. When

it met in January, 1864, the legislature called for a constitutional convention, which sat from April to September except for recesses during Early's Raid and the Republican national convention held in Baltimore in July. The document that emerged did so over the protests of rural proslavery delegates. It radically changed the balance of power in Maryland by basing representation in the House of Delegates not on total population as rural, heavily slaveholding districts wished, but on the size of the white population. It also instituted a strict loyalty oath — election judges had the discretion to decide whether a voter was taking it in good faith — and disqualified from voting or holding office any who had supported the Confederacy in deed or in speech. Families who sent clothing, food, or letters to their sons in Confederate service were thereby disqualified. The convention then brazenly applied those powers to the ratification process itself. In the fall of 1864, with troops voting heavily and as many as two-thirds of Maryland voters disqualified for disloyalty, the Constitution of 1864 passed. However controversial, it put a laudable end to one overreaching evil: Maryland became the first former slave state in the Union to abolish slavery.

THANK GOD FOR MARYLAND FREEING HER SLAVES.

Above: "Arrival of Freedmen and their Families at Baltimore, Maryland — an Every Day Scene." Because Baltimore had long been known for its large and strong free black population, vast numbers of recently freed slaves from the upper South made their way to the city in search of jobs and a new life. Frank Leslie's Illustrated Newspaper, *September 30, 1865.*

Left: "Freedom." This woodcut from Harper's Weekly, *December 3, 1864, is indicative of changing public opinion in the North. As the war progressed, ending slavery became a more popular war aim. The caption below this romantic image reads, "Thank God for Maryland Freeing Her Slaves."*

"View of Transparency in Front of Headquarters of Supervisory Committee for Recruiting Colored Regiments, Chestnut Street, Philadelphia, In Commemoration of Emancipation in Maryland, November 1, 1864."

When Maryland formulated a new state constitution in 1864 it became the first former slave state to abolish slavery — an act that was celebrated on the national level by a notice in Harper's Weekly and in Philadelphia by the painting of a three-story, back-lit "transparency" hung in front of the city's recruiting office for colored troops. The canvas, which showed gallant black soldiers in action at the Petersburg Crater and at Fort Wagner, noted that twelve thousand colored soldiers from Maryland were now at the front fighting for the Union, heralded Maryland's tradition of religious freedom, and proclaimed that Maryland's antislavery stand pointed the way toward "a regenerated South."

THE RESULT OF THE FIFTEENTH AMENDMENT,
And the Rise and Progress of the African Race in America and its final Accomplishment, and Celebration on May 19th A.D. 1870.

"The Result of the Fifteenth Amendment and the Rise and Progress of the African Race in America and its final Accomplishment, and Celebration on May 19th A.D. 1870." Ten thousand blacks marched — and ten thousand more lined the streets — in Mount Vernon Place, celebrating their newly won right to vote. At the head of the column is a black veterans' unit, sporting colorful Zouave uniforms. Border vignettes show heroes of the abolition movement and the Civil War as well as scenes depicting black troops in action and the importance of education and religion. Frederick Douglass was the featured speaker, remembering that thirty-five years before he had been working as a slave in Talbot County, but now he could stand before the crowd as "an American citizen."

It is well that Baltimore should be selected as the city in which the enfranchised people of the nation should celebrate the great jubilee of freedom. Other cities have had their processions and rejoicings, but by common consent the task of making the grand demonstrations which should give expression to the gratitude and the joy of the whole of the colored people of the whole nation was awarded to Baltimore.

Baltimore *American*, May 20, 1870

He [Rebel officer] said 'Well Sirs I can tell you that you are in the midst of thousands of Rebels' and he said it in a very threatening way which I thought was meant to intimidate– Father then said 'Well sir I can just tell you that I am a Union man.'

Frederick A. Shriver of Union Mills to Wirt Shriver,
July 4, 1863

Frederick S. Wilson, of Frederick County, was at Georgetown University when the Army of Northern Virginia moved north for the second time, in the summer of 1863. On June 16, at Boonsboro, Maryland, he enlisted in the 1st Maryland Cavalry and remained with the unit until it surrendered on April 19, 1865. He then returned to Frederick County. Frederick D. Shroyer.

Innocence Lost

I suppose the split twixt us and Uncle's folks will soon become as hard to unite as the Union.

Wirt Shriver to Frederick A. Shriver, July 13, 1863

The character of the war changed after Antietam. Survivors could describe it as a "hard fight" with heavy losses but the fact was that they had begun to accept heavy loss within their ranks. In December, 1862, when General Burnside, then in command of the Army of the Potomac, ordered a series of futile assaults against Marye's Heights outside Fredericksburg, Virginia, well-protected Confederates shot them down by the thousands. Six months later, on July 3, 1863, many of those same Confederates, led by Gen. George Pickett, moved across a mile-wide valley toward Cemetery Ridge at Gettysburg. Crouched behind breastworks and a low stone wall, Union veterans of the nightmare below Marye's Heights prepared to take their revenge, chanting, "Fredericksburg! Fredericksburg!" Of the fourteen thousand Rebels making Pickett's charge, only about half returned. It would grow worse — in the Wilderness and at Spottsylvania Court House in the summer of 1864, and reach a bloody apex at Cold Harbor, Virginia, where assaulting federals lost seven thousand men in less than twenty minutes.

This was not the war for which men had volunteered, a quick, colorful affair with opportunities for distinction. It was deadly, grim, and apparently endless. The means of waging it, and the men who formed into lines and marched into likely, if not certain, death reflected the change. Blacks, never accepted as equals by Northern soldiers, were accepted as cannon fodder. Civilians in the wrong place at the wrong time were no longer spared.

Marylanders caught up in the war suffered these hardships with everyone else, in battles large and small, far away or close to home.

CHARGE OF MARYLAND INFANTRY (C.S.)
Gettysburg July 3rd 1863.

"Charge of Maryland Infantry, (C.S.), Gettysburg, July 3rd, 1863." Lithograph by Allen C. Redwood.

From July 1 to July 3, 1863, the armies fought the greatest battle of the war at the crossroads town of Gettysburg, Pennsylvania. Had Lee won it, the war might have ended in Confederate victory, and for the first two days it looked as though he might have victory in hand. After driving back scattered Union regiments on July 1, Lee the next day launched a series of attacks on the Union "fishhook" on Cemetery Ridge, the Round Tops, and Culp's Hill. The attacks were uncoordinated and began late in the afternoon. At twilight, about 8 P.M., four Confederate brigades, including Steuart's Brigade with the 2d Maryland Infantry, crossed the valley of Rock Creek and climbed the rugged, rocky, heavily wooded slopes of Culp's Hill. Although the Union lines had been weakened as Gen. George G. Meade sent reinforcements to beat back the attacks on the other side of his line, the troops left in the entrenchments on Culp's Hill put up a furious defense. Nevertheless, as darkness fell, after two hours of fighting so intense that men

could not be heard above the noise, the Confederates pushed a few men, among them a handful of Marylanders, to the top of the hill, where they remained overnight.

The next morning the fight resumed. To rescue their stranded elements, the Confederates at first light mounted another assault by the Maryland infantry, several regiments of Virginians, and a North Carolina regiment. Union lines had been strengthened during the night and the assault was cut down as it crossed several hundred yards of open ground. The Maryland infantry, sheltered by woods, fought their way closest to the Union breastworks before they were beaten back. The battle ended about 10:30 A.M. Among the dead lay Private Wesley Culp, 2d Virginia, who had died within sight of the house in which he was born.

A story told after the war to a Confederate participant in the battle illustrates how vicious the fighting was, and how determined its veterans had become. After the Southerners had withdrawn, a wounded Rebel sat up

[T]here was fighting done in front of Aunt Rebecca's house also, a dead Rebel was found on their pavement afterwards and one mortally wounded in their alley.

Frederick A. Shriver to Wirt Shriver, July 4, 1863

"The Dead on Culp's Hill." Alexander Gardner, July, 1863.

unsteadily, and when he realized where he was picked up his rifle and began loading it. In front of him, Union soldiers took aim, an officer waiting to give the order to fire. The Confederate shouted that he would rather be dead than be made a prisoner. With that he put the muzzle to his head and with the ramrod pushed the trigger.

A little more than four hours later, fourteen thousand Southerners set off across a mile of open ground toward Cemetery Ridge with the same grim determination. With the Union flank on Culp's Hill secure, federal artillery and infantry tore huge gaps in the Confederate battle lines. A few Rebels reached the small stone wall, the "bloody angle," on Cemetery Ridge—only to be killed or captured. The rest withdrew, leaving behind nearly seven thousand dead and wounded men. Pickett's charge has since come to be known as the "high water-mark of the Confederacy."

Pvt. David Ridgely Howard, Co. A, 2d Maryland Infantry, C.S.A. The younger brother of James McHenry Howard, David lost his leg at Culp's Hill and spent some years in Canada after the war rather than take the oath of allegiance. This photograph, taken after the war, portrays the young man wearing a Confederate enlisted man's uniform and the Maryland cross botany. The photographer has cleverly positioned Howard's rifle to hide his missing leg. Hampton National Historic Site, National Park Service.

The dashing Capt. William Murray commanded the Maryland Guard City Militia in Baltimore during the tumultuous days after the April 19, 1861, riot. He quickly left for Virginia, where he organized many of his former men into a company. In May it joined the 1st Maryland Infantry as Company H. In 1862 he formed in Richmond the first company of the 2d Maryland Infantry. While commanding the right of the line on July 3, 1863, in the advance on Culp's Hill, he was killed instantly by a volley of Union musketry. After the war his men erected a special memorial to him in the Confederate section of Loudon Park Cemetery.

There came little puffs of smoke, a rattle of small arms, the sensation of a tremendous blow and I sank forward on my horse, who ceased his prancing . . .

Henry Kyd Douglas

"Good Deeds Rarely Do Harm"

With the 2d Maryland charging up Culp's Hill on the morning of July 3 was Henry Kyd Douglas. Anxious to help the isolated men on the crest, he offered to lead one of the brigades himself and so was on horseback, sword pointed up the steep slopes, when several Union sharpshooters emerged from the woods "a couple of hundred yards up the heights" and trained their rifles on him. "I fancied I could look down the barrels and I fancied also they were large enough to crawl into," he recalled after the war. "There came little puffs of smoke, a rattle of small arms, the sensation of a tremendous blow and I sank forward on my horse, who ceased his prancing . . . several officers seized my horse and held me on him, taking my sword from my right hand."

The ball struck Douglas below the left clavicle, driving bits of his uniform into the wound and temporarily paralyzing his left arm. He was taken to the rear, then by ambulance a few miles from Gettysburg to the farmhouse of Henry Pickering, where other wounded Confederates lay in the barn. Placed in the parlor, Douglas asked to be moved out of the way, but Mrs. Pickering, "a tall, slender, young-looking woman, bearing the sweet likeness of her character upon her face" stooped down to quietly assure him that the parlor was little used and she preferred him there. A Union cavalry officer took his parole and those of his wounded men.

For two weeks he remained in the house, making friends with the Pickering children, who called him "the big Rebel," and mending without infection. So well treated were the Confederates that when sufficiently recovered, "a number of them took his [Pickering's]

wagon and horses, hauled in his wheat from the field and stacked it where he wished it." Douglas's mother and sister arrived from their home near Sharpsburg, having met "no disagreeable incident, nor a discourteous word" along the way. "They came and went in absolute safety and when blocked by artillery or cavalry or wagon trains they were helped on their way."

The Confederates and Douglas's family at the Pickerings did not go unnoticed. There were "intimations from neighbors of a different stamp that such kindness toward the enemies of the Union was scarcely consistent with strict loyalty and that there might be a day of reckoning." Pickering ignored these veiled threats and was soon elected surveyor of the county. In that capacity, he took part in laying out the battlefield.

In mid-July, Douglas was moved to a seminary hospital—where he was befriended by the female nurses and covertly taken on night walks into Gettysburg, even to taverns. A month later he was shipped to the harsher discipline of West Buildings Hospital in Baltimore. When sufficiently recovered, he asked that his parole be honored and he be released from confinement, in as much as he had done a similar favor for a Union officer in the Shenandoah Valley. The War Department, and Gen. Robert C. Schenck, then commanding troops in Baltimore, refused, and Douglas soon found himself with 1,500 other Confederate officers in the prison camp on Johnson's Island, in Lake Erie, "hardly the place Southerners would select as a winter resort," he observed wryly. Johnson's Island, he added, "was just the place to convert visitors to the theological belief of the Norwegian that Hell has torments of cold instead of heat."[1]

Frederick native Dr. Lewis H. Steiner (below) was teaching chemistry at the Maryland College of Pharmacy in Baltimore when war broke out. He joined the U.S. Sanitary Commission — a volunteer organization dedicated to the physical and spiritual care of Union soldiers — and in 1863 was appointed chief inspector with the Army of the Potomac. He vividly described his experiences as a battlefield surgeon at Antietam and Gettysburg in two published reports and a brief history of the commission. At the close of the war Steiner was chosen president of the Frederick County school board, where he devoted himself to providing school facilities for black students. A Republican, he served in the state senate from 1871 to 1883. In recognition of his experience as a scholar and educator, the directors of the new Enoch Pratt Free Library in 1884 appointed Steiner its first librarian. Daniel Carroll Toomey.

Right: U.S. Sanitary Commission Hospital Tents, Gettysburg, 1863.

"The Baltimore Sanitary Fair at the Maryland Institute." From Frank Leslie's Illustrated Newspaper, *May 14, 1864. Baltimoreans raise funds and supplies for Union army hospitals. Peale Museum, Baltimore City Life Museums.*

A Marylander in Tennessee

Exerpts from the Diary of an Unknown Union Officer from Baltimore at the Battle of Knoxville, November 1863

After the Union catastrophe at Chickamauga in September, 1863, Ulysses S. Grant, Union commander in the West, placed Gen. George H. Thomas in command of the Army of the Cumberland, then trapped and short of food in Chattanooga. Supplies and men soon arrived from the Army of the Potomac, and William T. Sherman brought in elements of the Army of the Tennessee. As Grant, Sherman, and Thomas prepared to break through Braxton Bragg's Confederates entrenched on the heights above Chattanooga, Gen. Ambrose Burnside moved through the mountains of eastern Kentucky and Tennessee to occupy Knoxville. Although Burnside hardly threatened Bragg on the heights overlooking Chattanooga, the Confederates sent Gen. James Longstreet's twelve thousand veterans with additional infantry and cavalry to dislodge him. On November 23–25 Union troops in Chattanooga broke out and smashed Bragg with spectacular victories at Lookout Mountain and Missionary Ridge. Four days later Longstreet's men reached Knoxville, and a long, grinding fight — typical of what the war had become — began.

16th Monday. Arrived at Campbell's Station about 9 a.m. Our Cavalry skirmishing with his advance all night. About 10. a.m. he pushed so hard that we were forced to give him battle. At 10.30. we engaged him with Infantry. Our Regt was engaged about 45 m[inutes] and was withdrawn on account of our ammunition giving out. While we were falling back the rebs got around our flank pouring several volleys of musketry into us, though without much affect. Casualties were few. Private Malcolm Johnston of A Co. was missing. Maj. John M. Saintmyer played the coward, leaving the regiment while it was engaged, and reporting as captured, got on his horse and went to Knoxville. The engagement was kept up until night when we fell back to Knoxville, rebel's following us closely. Weather clear, roads almost impassable.

17th Tuesday, arrived at Knoxville at 6.30 a.m. Cavalry skirmishing commenced about 9 a.m. Our regt was formed in the rear of a battery. At 11. a.m. fireing was quite Brisk. The Brig was formed. Co A & F of our regt was deployed as skirmishers on the RR The rest of the Brig went to work throwing up rifle Pitts. Weather foggy.

18th Wednesday. fireing commenced at daylight was relieved from Picket at night and marched into town, and detailed to pull down houses which was in the way of our Batteries. . . .

19th Thursday. fireing commenced Briskly at daylight at 8. a.m. we fell in line and marched into the rifle pits. Co A & F, I were sent to dam up a creek, about 11 a.m. our caval[ry] was withdrawn, the enemy strengthening his lines, worked his way down into a wood about 8 hundred yards of our pits, driving our men from the Creek. Co A & F then went to work under fire and dug their pits. Lt. Moor Co. C. was wounded in the side while standing near the Pit. Our Pickets not having any protection suffered greatly from the sharp shooters. Weather clear.

20th Friday. firing commenced at daylight to day our Pickets have protection having dug themselves pits during the night. Priv. McMillen was killed while on Picket in the rifle Pits. detail of sharp shooters was sent down to a flour mill in the town, about 6. P.M. the rebels opened a Battery on the 13th Indiana Battry but were soon quieted by the boys. Lieuts Lilly & Boldger played the coward. As soon as the first shell was thrown they ordered the Picket to fall back and skedaddled into camp, creating almost a panic, causing several Houses to be burned by the incendiary Dept. They were ordered before Genl. Burnside and put under arrest, and charged with cowardice and falsehood and Disobedeance of Orders. Maj. Saintmyer was also put under arrest. . . . At Campbell's Station was detailed for Picket had to take up the line under fire the detail was marched into the rebel lines by the officer of the Picket. Weather Rainy.

A Lieut jumped into one of the embrasures and cried Surrender you damded Yankees he was blown to atoms by a charge of grape and cannister.

21st Saturday. fireing commenced at daylight in the Rifle Pits. was relieved from Picket by Lt. Flackenstein. Weather rainy.

22nd. Sunday. fireing commenced at daylight in the Pits. had inspection. The rebs opened their Baty at 5.30 P.M. threw a few shells in the City without doing any damage. The Baty which opened to day was part of Alexandrias Battalion. He had in position in front of our Div Two (2) Napoleons and Four (4) 24 lb Howitzers. Received this information from a negro who belonged to the Batt. Weather clear.

23rd Monday. Fireing commenced at daylight. Priv Wm. Cross was slightly wounded by a musket ball while standing near the Pits. About 8 P.M. the Rebels charged our Picket line and gained possession of some houses on the outskirts of the Town. The incendry Dept. set fire to a number of Dwellings, and blew up the arsenal, also burning the car house. They threw a few shell. Their range was bad. Picket fireing was kept up all night. Weather clear.

24. Tuesday. fireing at daylight. 44 Ohio charged the rebels out of the Town we then took up our old line. Casualties few on our side. in the Pits. Weather cloudy with rain at intervals.

25. Wednesday firing commenced at daylight. Wolford's cavalry went out on our left, had brisk skirmish destroyed the rebel pontoon Bridge and captured 30 Prisoners. Lieut Flackenstein put under arrest for trying to bribe the surgeon to give him a certificate of disability. A court was convened to try the Maj. and Lts F, L, & B. in the pits. Weather clear & cold.

26th. Thursday. firing commenced at daylight. Received orders to be ready to move at a moment's notice. . . . Weather clear & cold.

. . .

28th. Saturday firing commenced at daylight. In the Pits. Weather rainy. A dash was made on our line at night but repulsed.

29th. Sunday. The Rebels thought to try the Strength of our works. At 2 a.m. a Brigade of South Carolinians charged our lines, . . . and flanking our line on the left. One man of our Regt was mortally wounded and 30 taken Prisoners. At 3 a.m. I took charge of our line of Pickets. About 4 a.m. a Brig of Georgians supported by a Brig of South Carolinians made a charge on fort Sanders. Gallant was the charge but gallantly were they repulsed.

They planted their battle flag on the Parapet of the fort three times. A Lieut jumped into one of the embrasures and cried Surrender you damded Yankees he was blown to atoms by a charge of grape and cannister. Owing to the density of the fog and partly to the military skill in making the charge the guns of the fort could not be brought to bear on them, but Benjamin soon remedied this evil by cutting the fuses of the shell and using them as hand grenades, creating a havoc in their ranks. In vain did the officers try to rally their panic stricken men. The men couldn't see it. They had no notion of being hurled to destruction by telegraph. At the time of the charge on the Fort a second attempt was made by a Brig. of North Carolinians to . . . drive in our line of Picket, but with not quite as much success as the first. A few shots from our Pickets scattered them. Shelling was quite brisk on both sides. Rebel shells from the battery in our front fall short. Long will Burnside's wire be remembered by Longstreet's command. A Rebel Lieut that was captured was interrogated as to how he got so muddy. He replied that he had been caught in a damned Yankee wire trap. The trap alluded to by the Lt. was telegraph wire intertwined arround stumps near the Fort, which caused them to stumble into the ditch.

. . .

At 12. m. a flag of truce was sent to them requesting them to bury their dead and to exchange wounded which was done. It was a novel sight to see the two armies mingle together.

We learned that Longstreets force was three corps, he having been reinforced by Buckner by 6,000 men on the 27th. At 7. P.M. a gun was fired announcing the truce ended. Weather clear.[2]

Early's Raid

In July, 1864, as Union armies pressed toward Richmond, Confederate leaders hatched a daring plan. Rebel agents in Baltimore, Washington, and Southern Maryland would coordinate with Confederate naval forces to attack the prison camp at Point Lookout, Maryland, and free its seventeen thousand prisoners. Lee sent word of the plan to Gen. Jubal Early, commanding Stonewall Jackson's old Army of the Valley, with instructions to launch a third invasion of Maryland from the Shenandoah Valley. A Confederate army could move swiftly out of the Valley, cross the Potomac into Maryland, and march southeast to threaten and possibly seize lightly-defended Washington itself. If Grant reinforced the capital, Lee could then lash out at the weakened Union lines around Richmond.

When Confederate columns entered Maryland, Baltimore's citizens rushed to barricade the streets. This engraving was made in July 1863.

"Old Jube," or "Jubilee," as Early's men called him, wasted no time. He frightened one Union army up the Kanawha Valley, and sent another scurrying to the safety of the heights above Harper's Ferry. After feasting his army on Union supplies in Harper's Ferry, Early crossed the Potomac on July 6 with fourteen thousand men. Should the navy manage to free the men at Point Lookout — an entire Confederate corps — Early might accomplish the unthinkable and capture Washington.

Cutting wires and tearing up railroad track as they came, the Confederates moved so swiftly they plunged Maryland — and Washington — into a panic. Rebel cavalry demanded and received $20,000 in ransom from Hagerstown (the ransom demand had inadvertently lost a digit from the intended $200,000) and $200,000 more from Frederick. Rumors swelled Early's army to thirty thousand, far more than were available to defend the capital or Baltimore.

In the latter city, Union Gen. Lew Wallace reacted quickly. A once promising leader, he had lost favor with Grant at Shiloh and been sent to Baltimore, a backwater of the war, but his instincts in crisis were sound. Racing westward out the B&O to Frederick, he gathered all the militia and scattered army units he could find, 2,300 men in all, and hastily formed a line south of Frederick at the railroad junction to Baltimore and Washington, on the Monocacy River. Wallace realized his small force had no chance against Early, but Grant was sending reinforcements north, and to delay Early until they arrived would perhaps save Washington.

Speed was essential to the Rebel plan, and on July 9 Early pushed through Frederick and fell on Wallace's force — now reinforced to seven thousand — like a lightning bolt. In a sharp, four hours' fight at Monocacy he turned Wallace's flank, inflicted seven hundred casualties, and took a thousand prisoners, but strategically the damage had been done. Twenty-four hours passed as Early rested his exhausted army, and when it reached Washington, it was still not rested enough for an assault. News then reached him that the Point Lookout plot had been abandoned because the federals there had gotten word of it. Through his binoculars, Early could see Grant's veterans filing into the breastworks and decided against an attack. The following day, he repelled a Union sortie and turned back to Virginia, his bold opportunity, so near at hand, lost.

Harry Gilmor posed for this photograph after the war.

A soldier will make love wherever he goes, for the girls all expect it. They say, 'Poor fellow! he'll be killed, wounded, or captured soon, and we shall never see him again; let us give him all the pleasure we can.'

Harry Gilmor, *Four Years in the Saddle*

The Quintessential Cavalier

One of the more colorful sidelights to Early's Maryland incursion was Gilmor's Raid. In every respect, Harry Gilmor embodied the myth of the Southern Cavalier. His father, Robert Gilmor, Jr., as a young man had met Sir Walter Scott, author of the *Waverley* novels, and had built near Towson Town a house resembling a Scottish castle, Glen Ellen. There Gilmor grew up, learning the ways of a Baltimore County aristocrat and riding in jousting tournaments. In 1861 he was briefly detained by federal authorities for his strong Southern sentiments, and when released he crossed the lines to become a Confederate "irregular" cavalryman.

Irregulars, units on the edge of military organization but not quite guerrillas, were frowned upon by both sides. Robert E. Lee barely tolerated those in his command. But Gilmor's Marylanders, like many Marylanders in the Confederate army, were orphans with no state to feed, clothe, and arm them. For supplies they raided Union railroad and wagon trains. By such methods did Gilmor keep his command in the Shenandoah clothed and fed — sometimes in oysters, brandied cherries, and ice cream. His independence, good looks, and glamor attracted female admirers. "Say when, my dear *Sir*, will you permit me to make you an offer of my hand and heart?" a lovestruck young woman in Staunton had asked that spring. "My friends have always told me I was gentle, lovely, and amiable, and the greatest of inducements — I have a nice little fortune of my own." Gilmor's response was predictable. "A soldier *will* make love wherever he goes," he boasted, "for the girls all expect it. They say, 'Poor fellow! He'll be killed, wounded, or captured soon, and we shall never see him again; let us give him all the pleasure we can.'"[3]

In July 1864, attached to Bradley Johnson's cavalry brigade, Gilmor's troop moved north with Early, screening the Confederate infantry and burning railroad bridges north of Baltimore. At Cockeysville Gilmor was detached to march eastward and cut the Philadelphia, Wilmington, and Baltimore railroad bridge at Magnolia Station on the Gunpowder River.

His ride took him home. Wearing a long, black scarf and a black plume in his hat, and riding a coal-black horse, Gilmor reined in at the gates of Glen Ellen for a brief reunion with his family. On the morning of July 13 he marched on Magnolia Station, losing one man to an angry farmer along the way — the Confederate was fatally shot while trying to pull down a Union flag.

"The Raid into Maryland, Rebel Cavalry Occupying the Town of New Windsor." Frank Leslie's Illustrated Newspaper, *September 3, 1864. As soon as it became clear that Early would win the day at Monocacy, Bradley Johnson's cavalry moved into New Windsor, where he forced local shopkeepers to sell their wares for Confederate money. The raiders set fire to the railroad station and a railroad bridge, and Maj. Harry Gilmor and twenty men rode to Westminster to cut the telegraph lines. Striking terror into the hearts of loyal citizens, the cavalrymen swung southeastward to Cockeysville and burned the railroad bridges before moving through the Greenspring Valley to within a few miles of Baltimore.*

Though the bridge was guarded by Union infantry and a gunboat, Gilmor concealed his men on the north bank and seized the first train moving up from Baltimore with the intention of setting it afire and rolling it back over the bridge. Thwarted by an engineer who spiked the engine, Gilmor captured the second train and with it Maj. Gen. William B. Franklin of Cockeysville. That train he did run back over the bridge, temporarily setting it ablaze. All the railroads leading north out of Baltimore had now been cut.

Gilmor rode back toward Towson, intending to follow the main body of cavalry down Charles Street, where Johnston had already burned the home of Gov. Augustus Bradford in retaliation for the burning of the governor's mansion in Virginia. But friends with whom he stopped to share a glass of claret, at least so legend has it, warned him that Union cavalry squadrons were nosing out of Baltimore in search of raiders. The city, too, was ready, having called up its militia and barricaded the streets.

Gilmor put aside his intention of a brazen ride through the city and concentrated on a body of cavalry moving up York Road. In a bloodless night attack he drove them back and continued westward to Pikesville and south for a reunion with Early. Along the way Franklin escaped.

With the failure of Early's raid, Gilmor resumed carrying on the war in his own fashion. Later that summer when Confederate cavalry burned the town of Chambersburg, Pennsylvania, he defied orders and spared the house of a Union commander against whom he had fought in the Shenandoah—after meeting the general's wife. Wounded at Winchester in September, he recuperated not in a hospital but in the home of a widow friend and her two young nieces. In January, after escorting two different ladies to South Carolina, Gilmor returned to duty only to be captured near Moorefield, West Virginia. He spent the rest of the war as a prisoner.

"The Battle of Rickett's Ford"

T*he Civil War is said to have been a war of thirty-six major battles and "ten thousand fights." One of the latter occurred in October, 1864, as a band of ten Maryland Confederate cavalrymen under the command of one "Captain Bowie" from Prince George's County was returning to Virginia from a raid just south of Rockville. They had crossed the Potomac in search of boots and horses, but, being cavaliers, they had also come on a knight's errand — to gather finery for a lady's wedding. Late on the night of October 6, they stopped at a store on the road between Rockville and Washington. Three days later, A. G. Thomas, the store's clerk, recounted in a letter to his brother in Baltimore what happened — and Captain Bowie's fate.*

Dear Brother,

Thinking thee would like to hear from the front otherwise than through the newspapers, I write thee a brief dispatch. We had quite a nice time at our Literary Society — 5th Evening & I went to bed about 11 o'clock with quite a *headache*. At exactly 12 that night Uncle Gid hellooed upstairs to me saying there was some one on the porch that wanted to go into the store. (Arthur Stabler just happened to be staying with me all night.) I got up and put a few clothes on and went downstairs to see who it was. I did not expect to open the store that time of night so I took my little pistol down instead of the key. Upon opening the door a large man stared me in the face and wanted to know if I was the clerk of the store, and upon answering him he demanded the key of the store or for me to go down and open it. I then enquired who he was, where he came from, what he was doing here, and he said he was passing through the neighbourhood and wanted a good many things and that it was none of my business who he was. I told him he could not go into the store without telling me who he was. Well he said it was just a question with me, if I did not open the door he would break it down. I then told him to await there until I saw the proprietor of the store. After slipping upstairs and hiding the store money & watch (min[e]) which I had in bed, I awoke Arthur up & then left him to dress while I went up for Uncle All.

He got up a[nd] came down with his new shot gun & revolver. I then stirred up Joe Davis (a reb). We, Arthur, Joe Uncle All & I formed behind the store and marched around on them not knowing their number and asked what they wanted — but before we knew it 10 Rebs had surrounded us and to surrender was the only alternative to being shot. They captured Uncle A's arms but I threw mine behind a goods box and he only found a few chesnuts in my pockets which I *gave* the *sneak*.

We were all so closely watched that it was impossible to get off. Again the key was demanded: they soon found out I was the clerk that had left the door so they pitched into *me*. Arthur had hid the key so I could not produce it, but I could not satisfy them that I hadn't it, so they took me up into my room and searched it but *nary key*. [H]e took my fine boots and brought me down again to the Captain 'Bowie' who seized ahold of my arm and ordered a man to take hold of the other side and sent a third to his horse and got a rope & said he could get the key, but [nary] time. He took me around in the back yard and threatened to *hang this*, but I told him *hanging* would not get it out of me. He then asked where he could get in & I told him there were some windows on the back side that were not very strong so with the aid of Uncle Gid's axe the end windows on the N. side was opened then the door from the inside. We were all ordered in then and after getting lighted up (they had a candle) a confiscation of goods ensued. It is hardly worthwhile to say what kind of goods they took as they got a little of every thing and a *good deal* of *some things*. The Capt. had a list which called for [illegible]llasian Kid Gloves, white Belt, sash, slippers &c &c so we think a wedding was pending. Just before they left Arthur Stabler got out of the library window, ran over to H. Johnson & got a gun & pistol & went up by Wm. H. Farquhar's gate and as they passed he *fired* twice. One fellow yelled out and they hastened their speed. Half past one as soon as they left several of us scouted the neighborhood over and got together 17 men. Besides Arthur, Trail.

Uncle All who went to Rockville for troops, but could not get any as they had just been ordered off. The seventeen were as follows — Perrie Leizear, John Able,

[T]hree of the rebs rushed out upon Warwick & John Able [&] Sam Leizear with a yell we so often hear of when a charge is made. Shoot you s___ a _____!!! where upon John did shoot one fellows hat off.

Wm. H. Ent, Geo Tucker, John Osborn & Warwick Stabler, J. C. Gilpin, Eddie & Johnnie Thomas, C. G. Porter, S. P. Thomas, Geo. E. Brooke, F. Miller, Sam Leizear, Joe Davis & John Walker, &c. We tracked them through the county very well so they would drop a hat, shoe & bundle of [illegible] every little bit. Most of us had pistols. John Able & Ent had shot guns, heavily loaded, but we came upon our game rather unexpectedly. After crossing a small stream about 3 miles N. of Rockville those that were riding ahead saw where they turned out in a little skirt of thick pines and riding on about 30 yds found them laying down asleep. Part of us were ordered to dismount and charge upon them while asleep, but most of the company rode up the hill at a rapid rate right near where they layed and started them up leaving John Able & Osborn, Warwick & Sam Leizear, Ent & Johnnie & myself to bear the brunt of the fight. We walked up the hill to see what was to be done only leaving Warwick & John Able & co at the ford. Perrie Leizear seemed to think we had better go away and leave them until some cavalry came from Rockville. Uncle Joshua, Joe Davis & Eddie Thomas had been despatched at different times hurry them up (leaving us with 4 men). Just as John Osborn, Johnnie Thomas & I started down to the ford again to draw our boys off three of the rebs rushed out upon Warwick & John Able Sam Leizear with a yell we so often hear of when a charge is made. Shoot you s___ a _____!!! where upon John did shoot one fellows hat off. Warwick's revolver snapped & the Rebs fired several shots at them. John Osborn, Johnson, Ent & I ran down to their assistance but before we could relieve them they had fallen back up the road from which we came. The Rebs then siezed two of our horses that were hitched at the ford mounted and commenced *pursuit*. John Osborn, Johnnie T. & I being on the Infantry order and — having the centre to hold fell back in *good order* up the branch. We did some running that cant be surpassed in any engagement. But fortunately the Rebs followed those that had shot instead of us or they could have ridden over and shot us down. As those two fellows were following John Able & Warwick up the road (toward Rockville) John fired a second time at the one on John Osborn's horse knocking him off and shot the horse's eye out, then Capt. Bowie took it up and shot at John several times and just as he was passing by Old Ent who was concealed behind a pine bush let him have a whole load of buckshot in the face & upper part of the head which knocked him sky high. (The gun roared like a *Cannon*). Then our party was pretty well scattered some going one way and some another. We felt very uneasy until we got together again and heard that none of our men were hurt. This was about 8 1/2 oclock when the fight took place and we did not return to the field until about 1 — where we found two of our captured horses & three of theirs hitched, in their deserted camp, and 218$ worth of stolen goods that they had left. And after following a wagon track up to a house from the pool of blood in the road, we found Capt Bowie's dead body attended by his brother [Brune?] who stayed with it he did not die until 12 m. his brother we took prisoner and sent to Washington guarded by three of our company. F. Miller had a coffin prepared and he (Capt.) was sent to his father in Prince Geo. Co. next day.

Fifty years later, in the fall of 1914, A. G. Thomas wrote to one of the Confederate raiders, J. G. Wiltshire, a Baltimore doctor, recounting the incident and apparently reminding him of the stolen boots. Wiltshire replied wistfully:

Your itemized account for boots is an interesting document. As I look at it I am reminded of the [horrors] of war, & of the serious consequences that fall in the invasion of one's rights. Had Bowie followed my advice he in all probability would be alive today. I do not mean to beg the question; to the contrary. As for that I was equally guilty with the rest of the boys. Our raid on your uncle's store was a poor & ill advised move; Had we passed on we could have crossed the Potomac in safety.

"Point Lookout, Md. View of Hammond Gen'l Hospital and U.S. Gen'l Depot for Prisoners of War." Color lithograph by E. Sachse & Co., 1864. Originally established as a federal hospital in July, 1862, the facility at Point Lookout was planned to accomodate up to 1,500 men. After the battle of Gettysburg, however, the site was converted to a Confederate prison camp able to hold some ten thousand men in tents. Conditions at first were moderate, the prisoners' chief complaints being the cold and lack of food. Escape attempts were frequent, aided by the surplus blue U.S. regulation trousers sent by the quartermaster's office when filling clothing supply requests. But by early 1864 the number of prisoners had increased to more than twenty thousand, and conditions had deteriorated. The prisoners' tents can be seen at the upper right.

Point Lookout

To go into a prison of war is in all respects to be born over.

Sidney Lanier, Tiger Lilies, 1867[1]

One might expect that the fate of prisoners in a brothers' war would not be especially severe, and indeed in the war's first years that was the case. As with so many aspects of the conflict, the matter of dealing with prisoners had to be improvised. At first paroles of honor were freely extended and accepted, and exchanged prisoners might rejoin their units in a matter of days or weeks. By the summer of 1862 a cartel had formally worked out the process: a captain could be exchanged for a captain, privates for privates, and in the absence of the right body, sixty privates could exchange a general. Since prisons were to serve as but temporary lodgings until an exchange could be arranged, they, too, were improvised: a deserted slave pen in St. Louis, converted training camps like Camp Douglas in Illinois, a tobacco warehouse in Richmond overlooking a building whose sign read, "Libby."

But events soon upset these delicate workings. When Gen. Benjamin Butler hanged a man in New Orleans for tearing down the Union flag, Jefferson Davis promptly declared that no more Union officers would be exchanged until "Beast" Butler had been punished. The presence by 1863 of former slaves in U.S. service brought another angry Confederate response. Captured black troops and their white officers would be subject to the Southern states' laws regarding slave insurrection. The soldiers might be returned to slavery or put to death, their white officers were liable to be executed, but they would not be exchanged. The cartel began to break down. The numbers held in prison camps, and the number of camps, grew.

Following the battle of Gettysburg, federal authorities seeking a place to confine the thousands of Confederates wounded and captured there turned their eyes on Maryland. At Point Lookout in strongly pro-Southern St. Mary's County, a spit of land jutted into the juncture of Chesapeake Bay and the Potomac River. Before the war it had begun to gain notice as a small but attractive watering place for those seeking respite from a central Maryland summer. Army physicians, who understood that ventilation improved the chances of recovery from wounds or sickness, had built a hospital there to take advantage of its cooling breezes. All the site needed was the addition of administration buildings, guard barracks, and a palisade.

Arriving in Baltimore by train from Gettysburg field hospitals, the first Confederate prisoners watched angry guards drive away friends and sympathizers bringing food and water. One man, his leg still bleeding, witnessed guards on the upper story of the prison hospital on Pratt Street pelt with rotten eggs a group of ladies bringing food and clothing to him and his comrades.

From Baltimore, bay steamers carried the prisoners to Point Lookout, where guards inspected them on the dock and kicked into the bay any article of clothing or equipment with a "U.S." stamped on it. Some prisoners reported they were made to stand out all night over the water as the gentle breezes turned cold. The chill winds to which they were exposed were but harbingers of things to come: the government's, and Secretary of War Edwin Stanton's, policy regarding prisoners of war was about to change.

As the cartel foundered in the fall of 1863 — it would be another six months before Union commander Ulysses S. Grant called for a halt to exchanges altogether — growing numbers of federal prisoners strained already thin Confederate resources. In the grip of a tightening Union blockade, the South had little enough for its soldiers and citizenry. A drought in 1862 had left

Pvt. Edward Clagett, Company F, 2d Maryland Infantry, C.S.A., photographed while a prisoner at Point Lookout. Frederick D. Shroyer.

withered crops, and by March, 1863, the Army of Northern Virginia was on half rations. Civilians fared no better. In April, armed with knives, desperate wives of Confederate soldiers marched through Mobile, Atlanta, Salisbury, and Richmond in search of food and clothing. At each store they asked the price of flour, declared it was too high, and looted the inventory. Moreover, reports of mistreatment of prisoners had begun to filter out of Southern camps, and demands from an angry Northern public that harshness be returned in kind rained down on the administration. In the spring of 1864 the South voluntarily returned some severely wounded and ill prisoners. Stanton had them photographed and examined in Congress and declared, "There appears to have been a deliberate system of savage and barbarous treatment and starvation" in the South. Although Union prisoners in Confederate hands merely suffered the same severe shortages of food and clothing that plagued the entire South, Stanton ordered the rations given Confederate captives — up to that point Union army rations — cut by 20 percent. Federal camp commanders sometimes withheld more and arbitrarily withdrew comforts that were readily available.[2]

Together with President Lincoln, Stanton visited the new prison camp at Point Lookout two days after Christmas, 1863. If his intention was to make sure the prisoners were uncomfortable but able to survive, he must have been pleased. The men confined in the one-thousand-foot walled square — named the "bull pen" — did not live in wooden barracks but faced autumnal Chesapeake gales in bell-shaped Sibley tents rejected by the Union army. Up to sixteen men huddled on the floor of each, an area about fifteen feet square. Although the winter of 1863–64 was bitterly cold, wood was strictly rationed. The amount of pine brush three men could carry sometimes had to heat a tent for a week — in January. One prisoner estimated the wood ration as "about a cord of green pine to one thousand men for five days." He added, "It was mockery."

Hardened campaigners though they were, the weather was almost more than the prisoners could bear. It was "so coal that we all had to lye down and rap up in our Blankets to keep from freezing for we had no wood to make us a fire," wrote a North Carolinian in mid-February, 1864. The soldiers kept warm by "spooning" three to a blanket. "One morning," a veteran wrote later,

> I notice a pale-faced soldier lying opposite me . . . and I notice his old shoes were sockless, and his tattered pantaloons reached to a few inches below his knees, leaving a bare and naked space. I just reached over . . . and took hold of his leg, which was just as cold as an icicle, and he did not awake. . . . he had become so hardened to cold and hunger that it was a second nature.

Guards routinely confiscated extra clothing and blankets the prisoners managed to accumulate. A prisoner fortunate enough to receive from his family a new coat or shoes first had to turn in his old ones.

At the time of Stanton's visit, though the 20 percent cut was yet to come, the prisoners' food was already too little. "The 25th was Christmas day," wrote a North Carolinian at the time of Lincoln's visit, "and it was clear and coal and I was boath coal and hungry all day onley got a peace of Bread and a cup of coffee for Breakfast and a small Slice of Meat and a cup of Soop and five Crackers for Dinner and Supper I had non." In June, 1864, the prison stopped issuing coffee and tea and cut all rations. A prisoner captured in April, 1865, reported the men were so hungry "they would eat almost anything they could pick up outside from the sewers; potato peelings, cabbage stalks, or most any kind of refuse that hardly the cattle would eat."

Another problem was water. It came from two slow-drawing wells inside the prison compound — five feet above sea level at its highest point — and was so tainted "with some mineral as to offend every nose, and induce diarrhoea in almost every alimentary canal," one man complained. "It colors every thing black in which it is allowed to rest, and a scum rises on the top of a vessel if it is left standing during the night."

Survival dominated the thoughts of prisoners from dawn roll call until the blowing of taps. The wise disciplined themselves to make their food last from one day at noon, when it was issued, until the next, but as men slowly wasted their will eroded. Frequently the two or three ounces of bacon or beef, the half loaf of bread, or the crackers disappeared in a few moments, leaving the soldier to contemplate the next twenty-four hours. To supplement their rations they sold to the guards intricate rings sculpted from buttons, chains of gutta percha, or figures whittled from bone. They volunteered for wood-cutting and labor details for the extra issue of food and caught fish, crabs, and oysters. They "flanked" the rules: dead men answered the roll and picked up rations; the agile ducked from one line to the next to receive two issues. But there was never enough food. The men began to catch and eat rats, and when a long-dead seagull washed up on shore one prisoner ate it on the spot.

Friction between guards and prisoners was inevitable, and reports of Southern atrocities added to the guards' ill will and rear-echelon nervousness. No sooner had the first men from Gettysburg arrived when a guard shot one in the head for looking through the plank wall of the enclosure. The prisoners thereby learned that the shallow trench fifteen feet from the wall was a true "deadline": anyone crossing it, or simply too near it, risked being shot. Soon after, a captain emptied his revolver into a crowd of prisoners that had gathered too closely around him near the gate, wounding five.[3]

Tension increased when a regiment of U. S. Colored Troops from North Carolina took up guard duty. One Kentucky officer, apparently slightly drunk, requested whiskey of a white New Hampshire sergeant and on being refused informed the federal that he was "a fit subject to associate with them," indicating the black sentries. The sergeant drew his revolver and promptly shot the Kentuckian dead. Prisoners suffering from diarrhea often ran afoul of angry former slaves who nightly patrolled the compound in pairs. According to numerous prisoners' accounts, the guards threatened them, made them run to the nearest wall and back, or had themselves carried about on the sick men's backs.

On April 18, 1864, word reached the camp of the massacre at Fort Pillow, a small Union post on the Mississippi. In an excess of bitterness, Confederate cavalry commander Nathan Bedford Forrest had apparently applied the laws of slave insurrection to the surrendered black garrison. That night at Point Lookout, a black sentry shot and killed a sick prisoner sitting on a tub outside his tent. A few nights later another sentry fired his rifle into a tent, prompting the camp's sergeant-major to plead with the commandant "to preserve us against the vindictiveness of certain of the colored troops who guard us." The shootings continued sporadically—one man was shot in the head in broad daylight while whittling—throughout the spring and summer of 1864.[4]

There were other hardships. The sun's glare off water, white tents, and sand temporarily blinded many. Though they bathed in the Chesapeake, prisoners could not escape the deadly summer fevers. A Virginian, who from the hospital roof could see his native Westmoreland County on the Virginia shore, wrote of a man dying of cholera "only two minutes after taken." Those who entered the hospital seemed to come out only for burial in the "Peach Orchard"—as the Gettysburg veterans named the cemetery. Of the approximately fourteen thousand prisoners in the camp, 250 or so died each month of sickness, and in the summer when the camp population reached nearer twenty thousand, that number quadrupled.

With some daring exceptions, few escaped. Early's raid in July, 1864, briefly exhilarated the camp and brought resignation thereafter. Some men took the loyalty oath and were released. Others enlisted to fight Indians in the West. In February, 1865, many of those captured at Gettysburg were finally paroled and sent home, too weak and broken to be of any use to the Confederacy. Not until June, after Appomattox, were the last prisoners released. In all, 3,389 prisoners died at Point Lookout, a monument to a war turned hard.[5] None of the survivors ever forgot—or forgave it.

A Man of Letters at Point Lookout Prison

While serving as a signalman aboard a blockade runner, Sidney Lanier was captured in 1864 and spent time at Point Lookout. At the initial inspection he managed to conceal in his sleeve his beloved flute, with which he amused himself and his tent mates. More useful was the gold a friend had smuggled in his mouth for it proved to be the means of their release four months later. Lanier also managed to keep the working draft of a novel he had begun in 1863. In it, he offered a description of his arrival at the Point.

. . . the stature of the men and the burning of their passions remained the same inside the prison as out of it, only the objects of these passions and exertions were immeasurably diminished in number and dignity. . . . this was the terrible feature in the prison-changed behavior of his old army friends. They did not crowd to shake joyful hands with him and hear the news from outside, but met him with smiles that had in them a sort of mournful greasiness, as if to say: Ah, old boy, mighty poor eating in here! Their handshakes were not vigorous, their souls did not run down and meet Philip's at the finger-tips. How could they? These same souls were too busy in devising ways and means to quiet the stomachs and intestines, . . .

Like so many of the captured Confederates, Lanier managed humor in the face of privation.

Passing a row of small A tents presently, the corporal looked at his book.

"Tent fifteen; think there's four men in it. Let's see." He thrust his head into the low opening. "How many in here?"

"'Bout a million, countin' lice and all!" responded a voice, whose tone blent in itself sorrow, anger, hunger, and the sardonic fearlessness of desperation.

"Guess they want another man in, if you don't," said the corporal, with a pleasant smile.

Prisoners' longing for home sometimes turned to fantasy. Omenhausser entitled this humorous and bittersweet sketch, "The Rebel's Dream in Prison."

No. 1 Halt-dar white man, whar you guoine?
"   2 I'm going to urinate.
"   1 Whats dat?
"   2 I'm going to piss.
"   1 Dar you's done told two tale's about
*   it, now double quick back to your tent.*

No. 3. Get down on your knees and pray for Abraham Lincoln.
"   4 Oh Lord bless President Lincoln
"   3 Now pray for the United States.
"   4 Oh Lord! Bless the army and navy of
*   the United States.*
"   3 Now pray for de colored people.
"   4 Oh Lord have mercy on the niggers, no I mean
*   on the colored people and deliver them from bondage.*

"True Sketches and Sayings of Rebel Characters in the Point Lookout Prison, Maryland, by John J. Omenhausser (Prisoner of War)," 1865. Private John Omenhausser of the 46th Virginia Infantry was captured near Petersburg in June, 1864, and taken to the federal prisoner-of-war camp at Point Lookout, St. Mary's County. In forty-five watercolor sketches he recorded a wide variety of scenes depicting prison life — the lack of food, the anger of U.S. Colored Troops and their sometimes rough treatment of the prisoners, bartering for extra rations, and taking the oath of allegiance to gain release, as Omenhausser himself reluctantly did on June 9, 1865.

The Reb that never saw a crab.
No 1. Mister just smell this bugs breath its the
     sweetest thing you ever smelled.
" 2. Make the damn thing let loose, or I'll
     smash his brains out.
" 3. Ha! Ha! Ha! I wonder if that feller
     will smell any more bugs.

Cooked Crabs
No. 4. Mister I'll give you a big chew tobacco for
     this feller.
" 5. Mister are them things good to eat?
" 6. Yes! does you think I'd sell anything that
     wasn't good to eat.

No 1 Double quick sah, or I'll blow daylight through
     you, and if you tells de major, I'll shoot you de
     fust time I see's you.
" 2 Don't hurt me Mister and I'll toat you anywhere.

Doublequicking
No. 3 You man wid de red shirt double quick into
     line or I'll pop a cap at you.
" 4 Oh me! I'm so cold.
" 5 I'm nearly out of breath.

"The Assassination of President Lincoln at Ford's Theater on the Night of April 14, 1865," Harper's Weekly, *April 22, 1865.*

The Final Tragedy

At about ten o'clock on the night of April 14, 1865, as a jubilant North celebrated the surrender of Lee's army earlier in the week at Appomattox Court House, a lone figure ascended the back stairs of Ford's Theater in Washington and made his way to the private boxes, all but one of which were empty. The stage below was, too, empty, save for a lone actor playing Asa Trenchard, one of the hilarious characters in *Our American Cousin*, featuring the celebrated British actress, Laura Keene.

As the audience rocked with laughter at Trenchard's antics, a single shot rang out above them. The President slumped forward, and a slight, athletic man evaded the young army major accompanying the Lincolns and leapt to the stage. His spur caught in some bunting, causing him to land awkwardly, but with practiced Shakespearian timing he flourished a dagger and shouted, "Sic temper tyrannis!" Some recognized his elegant clothes, his "classic face, pale as marble, lighted up by two gleaming eyes . . . and surmounted by waves of curling, jet black hair."[1] Many in the audience knew him immediately as the actor, John Wilkes Booth. The moment of stunned silence quickly passed as Booth fled into the night and the president's guard, bayonets fixed, rushed belatedly into the theater to clear it of a crowd who could not leave fast enough.

At roughly that same instant, an ill Secretary of State William Seward and his sons were frantically fending off a huge, knife-wielding Confederate veteran. Lewis Payne, nee Lewis Thornton Powell, had joined a Florida regiment in 1861 at the age of seventeen. At Antietam he had learned of the deaths of two brothers serving with Nathan Bedford Forrest in Tennessee. Captured at Gettysburg on July 3 and sent to work as a nurse in West Building Hospital in Baltimore, he there met an attractive Baltimore girl. In October he escaped to join

Booth's capture and death as portrayed in Harper's Weekly, *May 13, 1865.*

Mosby's irregulars and in 1864 fought in the countless, bitter guerrilla battles in the Shenandoah, where Union troops sent to burn farmhouses often turned up dead in the road. Powell's reputation in such fighting was fearsome. Captured in the fall of 1864, he had taken the oath of allegiance and returned to Baltimore, where he had met John Wilkes Booth. After badly wounding the Secretary of State and leaving his entire house in ruins, Payne mounted his horse within sight of several Union soldiers and casually rode away.[2]

Booth's escape route from Ford's Theatre took him at a quicker pace into the Maryland countryside. He turned southward and made his way through Prince George's and Charles counties to the farm of Dr. Samuel Mudd, who set his broken leg, and eventually across the Potomac. He would be caught and shot—some claim he shot himself—in a tobacco barn on a Virginia farm ten days later, after the largest military manhunt in American history.

The assassination of President Lincoln has been described as the act of a madman, and perhaps it was. Friends had always claimed a dark streak ran through the Booths. The father, noted actor Junius Brutus Booth, had left a wife in England and taken another in America, settling on a farm near Bel Air, twenty-four miles northeast of Baltimore. He battled alcoholism and exhibited behavior that other farmers surely interpreted as insanity, once inviting everyone to the funeral of his closest friend, which turned out to be his horse. On tour in Natchez, he climbed a ladder, crowed like a rooster, and vowed not to come down until Andrew Jackson was again elected president. John Wilkes was the ninth of his ten children—three of whom died. Though charming and witty, and by most accounts a decent actor if not so great as his brother, Edwin, Wilkes was also known to brood and to drink heavily—sometimes a quart of brandy in two hours.

Yet the assassination, which began as a plan to kidnap and ransom Lincoln and revitalize Confederate fortunes, should also be viewed in the context of a bitterly divided Maryland. The Booths were slaveholders, and John Wilkes Booth would have entered the Confederate army had his mother not extracted a promise from him not to do so. Mary Surratt, the mother of John Surratt, one of the conspirators, had seen her other son, Isaac, join the rebels as had so many of her Southern

Maryland neighbors. The Surratts and Dr. Mudd were slaveholders who worked their slaves as late as 1863 and possibly 1864, when the State of Maryland, not the Emancipation Proclamation, freed them.[3] Like so many others in this divided state, the Booths and Surratts hated a government that took away their "rights" and "property." Arrested because of her son's involvement with Booth and because the conspirators were found to have met in her Washington house, Mary Surratt was thrown into the Old Capitol Prison, where she found a large number of other women prisoners, like her Confederate sympathizers and agents.[4] Unlike them, it was her fate, together with three other conspirators, to face the gallows.

The assassination did not provoke universal grief. In Baltimore, where photographers displayed photographs of Confederate soldiers in their windows, pictures of Booth sold for twenty-five cents — Lincoln's for a dime. Gen. Lew Wallace early in May, 1865, forbade the display or sale of either Confederate or Booth souvenirs (the order was revoked a few weeks later). Here and there men who proclaimed their approval of the assassination, or their hatred of Lincoln, were shot, usually by an aroused soldier or policeman. In Westminster, citizens had run the editor of the *Democrat* out of town some time before because of his anti-Lincoln language. When he unwisely returned after the shooting, a group of angry citizens came to his house. The editor fired into the crowd and wounded a man, whereupon the crowd beat him to death.[5] Nevertheless, when Lincoln's body lay in state in Baltimore en route to Springfield, crowds of mourners wearing black ribbons and badges turned out to pay homage to the fallen president.

Among the most popular of Booth's photographs, this picture was one of a series the actor had taken in 1862 for distribution to his admirers. After the assassination authorities copied it onto government wanted posters. In Baltimore, where Southern feelings ran high, entrepreneurs mounted and sold this same image in gilt-emblazoned frames.

Generals Wade T. Hampton (left) and Bradley T. Johnson (right) circa 1900. At war's end, Johnson settled in Richmond and in 1875 was elected to the Virginia senate. Returning to Maryland in 1879, he resumed his legal career and wrote the Maryland volume of the massive Confederate Military History. *Always active with Confederate veterans' organizations, he served as president of the Association of the Maryland Line and the Society of the Army and Navy of the Confederate States in the State of Maryland. When he died in 1903 he was buried in the Confederate section of Baltimore's Loudon Park Cemetery.*

Remembrance

In June, 1865, Frederick Douglass' son, Lewis, a sergeant-major in the 54th Massachusetts Infantry, found himself with elements of his regiment stationed in Royal Oak, Talbot County. One day he walked the eight miles to St. Michael's to meet an aunt and cousin he had never known. When word spread of his arrival, young Douglass wrote his parents, crowds of blacks surrounded him in the street and treated him like a lion.

But with his father's eye, he noticed other things about St. Michael's. It was "one of the worst places in the South" for a black. Whites, hoping to keep black labor cheap and plentiful, refused to sell land to the

. . . but we are cautious in our efforts to be friendly, being surrounded in Baltimore by so many idiots of our own state who pretend not to know Marylanders who had courage enough not to be intimidated by them into rebellion!

Brantz Mayer, April 3, 1866

freedmen. Local attitudes toward the former slaves had hardened after emancipation, and a black man who raised his voice in protest took his life into his hands.[1]

Indeed, although Maryland slavery had been a casualty of the war, the labor system and racial attitudes that had been its underpinning had not changed. Black "orphans" — from shattered homes or kidnapped from the fields — were bound out to farmers and planters and treated much like chattel. So widespread was the apprenticeship of orphans that in Baltimore criminal court judge and Radical Republican Hugh Lennox Bond waged a lonely war against it, drawing a good deal of hate mail in the process. Eventually his efforts and those of a few others ended the practice, but many of the old patterns persisted. Like Harriet Tubman's former husband, shot dead in the road in broad daylight, blacks found themselves unprotected amidst a hostile white population.

Maryland's physical loss was relatively small in a war that elsewhere had proved devastating. Of the forty thousand men in Maryland Union units, nine hundred fell in battle, many of those in the bloody fighting at Spottsylvania Court House, where the Maryland brigade took severe losses. Casualties among the approximately twenty thousand Confederate Marylanders are unknown, but the state did not experience the tragedies endured in Massachusetts, New York, Pennsylvania, Michigan, North Carolina, or Alabama. Some regiments, particularly in the South, suffered enormously high casualty rates. Since regiments were raised locally, much of a community's manpower could be killed or maimed in a deadly hour, say at Pickett's charge.

Neither were Maryland's factories, railroads, and commercial fleet destroyed as were properties in the South. Indeed, great Maryland fortunes gathered during the war. Enoch Pratt and Johns Hopkins filled army contracts. John Work Garrett identified the Union cause with his B&O Railroad and prospered accordingly. Farmers and former planters managed the transition to free, if sometimes coerced, labor without having seen their crops burned and livestock requisitioned.

But if Maryland's wounds were not as numerous, they were deeper and slower to heal. For it was here, as elsewhere in the Border States, that families, neighbors, colleagues, and friends, had been pitted against one another. In the long, bitter aftermath of war, Massachusetts would reconcile with South Carolina before Marylanders would forgive one another.

A state with divided loyalties, Maryland was hospitable if not fertile ground for the Grand Army of the Republic, a Union veterans' organization formed in Pittsburgh in September, 1866. The G.A.R.'s purpose was to memorialize the Union dead and strengthen social — and soon political — ties among those who had fought for the Union. The organization grew slowly, only thirty thousand by 1878, but thirteen of its posts were in Maryland, and Baltimore's Wilson Post No. 1 boasted the largest post hall in the nation in the Rialto building. In 1878 its members pledged in addition to aiding distressed companions and widows: "to protect the Constitution of the land, obey its laws, and uphold the Starry Banner as the emblem of unity, equal rights and privileges to all men, without regard to race, color or previous condition of servitude." A few years later, as sectional passions cooled and more Union veterans felt the need to keep memories of their sacrifice alive, the G.A.R. grew to 409,000 nationally.[2]

Returning Confederate veterans, facing the need to rebuild their fortunes, were slower to organize but, wherever possible, quick to exert their force politically. While most acquiesced in the decision at arms, they did not accept Unionist governments in their states and swiftly overturned them. Maryland was no exception. In 1866, with the blessing of Gov. Thomas Swann, former Confederates returned to the polls, elected a Democratic legislature, and a year later rewrote the state constitution in a convention at which not a single Republican was present. When in 1870 the Fifteenth

Left: The Confederate monument in Loudon Park Cemetery, ca. 1870. Below: Maryland Confederate veterans at the monument, ca. 1900. During the war, Union troops observed the burial in Loudon Park of a Confederate killed at Gettysburg. After the ceremony they moved in and arrested the males present.

Amendment gave blacks the right to vote, Maryland refused to ratify it.

The leaders of Maryland society, having largely cast their lot with the South and risen to distinction in its service, made their presence felt in other ways. Barely a year after Appomattox, Baltimore hosted "the greatest fair ever held" in that city as the Ladies' Southern Relief Association raised funds to aid the states of the former Confederacy. For two weeks the halls of the Maryland Institute were "thronged with beauty, fashion and wealth" as the ladies, who counted among their number "the best-known women in Baltimore," glided among tables heavy with "fancy articles," confectionaries, a "Jacob's Well: filled with lemonade," one of George Washington's parlor chairs, canes made from the wood of the *Merrimac*, oil paintings, an art gallery, a "Floral Temple," and a "Fortune Bower" with fortunes, flowers, birds, music box, and monkeys. With tickets at two dollars apiece they raised $162,000 for the Southern relief.

Southern relief efforts in Maryland also called upon a genteel antebellum social activity, the sport of jousting. Orators who earlier had charged the "knights" — equestrian gentry clad in medieval regalia who speared tiny rings with sharply pointed lances — with obeying the spirit of chivalry now sprinkled their speeches with odes to Southern womanhood. Money raised at these tournaments went to a variety of Southern causes, and the tournaments could be extravagant. At the 1869 tournament at Brooklandwood in Baltimore County, carriages reportedly clogged the roads for two or three miles, and Confederate heroes Joseph E. Johnston and P. G. T. Beauregard were in prominent attendance.[3]

Maryland Confederates returning to Baltimore also formed the Loudon Park Confederate Memorial Association to honor their dead. Late in 1861 a sanitary commission had selected Loudon Park for the burial of Union casualties, but in May, 1862, pro-Southern families had begun burying their sons in a prominent part of the cemetery, sometimes under the watchful eyes

Now a little insight into the way we do in Maryland: We have no ex-Confederate societies, but several large, strong, and active Confederate societies. We have never mixed in any manner with the other side — have no joint reunions, no joint banquets, no decoration or memorial days in common. In fact, we do not mix, we go our way and they go theirs. . . . We do not belong to that class of Confederates that believed they were right. We knew we were right in 1861, we knew we were right when the war closed, and we know today that we were right.

William H. Pope, Superintendent of the Maryland Line Confederate Soldiers Home, 1893

Left: Commandant's house, Maryland Line Confederate Soldiers Home, Pikesville, Md., ca. 1890. Below, veterans gather to pose at the gate to the home, ca. 1895.

of Union troops. In 1870 Confederate veterans commissioned Adalbert Volck to sculpt an imposing marble figure of a Confederate soldier. Crowning what became known as "Confederate Hill," the monument soon served as the focal point for the annual celebration of "Confederate Memorial Day," held in Maryland on June 6.

In 1871 Confederate veterans organized the Society of the Army and Navy of the Confederate States in the State of Maryland and set about obtaining the return of Maryland bodies from scattered battlefields and cemeteries, not an easy task. In the war's immediate aftermath, with ill-feeling at its highest, the federal government had steadfastly pursued a policy of honoring Union dead and neglecting Confederate. At places like Antietam, the latter were only given proper burial

when hogs rooted their remains from shallow battlefield graves. In three years the society succeeded in bringing seventy-six bodies to Confederate Hill. Eventually Confederate burials at Loudon Park numbered nearly 650, the last taking place in 1937. Union burials numbered 2,300.[4]

Concern for the care of ill or destitute Confederate veterans spurred the formation in 1880 of the Association of the Maryland Line, which appropriated in its title the claim to Maryland's military glory in the war. In 1888 the state turned over to them the Pikesville Armory (from whence Snowden Andrews had stolen artillery reports in the heady days of 1861) that they might render it into a home for comrades in poor health and down on their luck. In June, 1888, the Maryland Line

Maryland Confederate veterans put together this exhibit from the "Relic Hall" at the Maryland Line Confederate Soldiers Home in Pikesville for the Confederate Relief Bazaar held at the Fifth Regiment Armory in Baltimore, 1898.

Scenes from the 16th G.A.R. Encampment at Baltimore in June, 1882, from Frank Leslie's Illustrated Newspaper, *July 1, 1882. Above, fireworks over Federal Hill in Baltimore Harbor. Facing page, fireworks and dancing at Camp Agnus.*

Confederate Soldiers Home opened and by 1893 housed 139 men, with the state contributing heavily to their maintenance. It would close in 1932, when the last two veterans left to spend their remaining days in private homes. In those years, the armory became something of a Maryland Confederate shrine, its rooms furnished by contributions and named for heroes — William Murray, Isaac R. Trimble, Harry Gilmor.

With time and political adjustment, usually at the expense of Southern blacks, old wounds began to heal. The national administration of Republican Rutherford B. Hayes withdrew the last handful of occupation troops from the South in 1877 and by the mid-1880s ceased waving the "bloody shirt" — the tactic of capitalizing on wartime bitterness in congressional and campaign speeches. They promptly lost the election of 1884, and in Grover Cleveland the country inaugurated the first Democratic president since James Buchanan.

In this climate of reconciliation, Union and Confederate veterans' organizations that had been holding separate reunions and encampments in the 1870s found it possible, even joyful, to speak to one another. Gradually they began gathering on the battlefields where they had so desperately fought, meeting at Chick-amauga and Gettysburg to swap stories and make sometimes poignant discoveries. Faces on the other side of the campfire had once lain behind a breastworks or fixed bayonets in an oncoming battle line. Veterans appreciated shared hardship and bitter sacrifice; respect for the enemy, once unthinkable, became natural.

In June, 1882, the Grand Army of the Republic held its 16th National Encampment for the first time in a "southern city" — Baltimore — and invited Southern units to participate. Thousands filled the major hotels or camped at Sheutzen Park, named "Camp Agnus" after Baltimore *American* publisher and former Union general Felix Agnus. The city sported elaborate patriotic decorations put up by local businesses. President Chester A. Arthur and members of his cabinet arrived aboard a special coach provided by B&O president Garrett and joined the governor and the mayor. Other distinguished guests included members of the Supreme Court and Frederick Douglass.

A grand parade wound from the foot of Broadway north and west to Monument Square, ending at the reviewing stand at City Hall. Maryland national guard units stepped off, followed by members of Maryland's

CAMP AGNUS

twenty-one G.A.R. posts, five of them U.S.C.T. veterans. The 6th Massachusetts, whose earlier arrival in 1861 had caused a riot, marched, according to *Harper's*, "as upon red roses." Sixty-six veterans from Duryee's Zouaves, erstwhile occupiers of Federal Hill, paraded in their blue-braided jackets, baggy pants, and red fezzes. Later at the Academy of Music they performed their colorful bayonet drill accompanied by a "living tableaux." (One scene, "Shaking Hands over the Bloody Chasm," featured a "bevy" of local children and aptly symbolized the encampment's theme — the healing of old wounds.) After the parade veterans and the public journeyed out to Camp Agnus for a concert of military music, a campfire and picnic, and a grand display of fireworks. The next day, four steamers conveyed the guests to Tivoli, one of the favorite pleasure grounds on the bay, for a festive afternoon and supper of Maryland delicacies. They returned in time for fireworks on Federal Hill and a grand ball at Camp Agnus, where the dancing began at 10 P.M.

The encampment drew praise in *Harper's Weekly* and *Frank Leslie's Illustrated Newspaper* for the harmony it demonstrated, though not every former Confederate had been reconstructed. The notoriously pro-southern Bendann's had as a window display a recent photograph picturing twenty-eight of the thirty-five survivors of William H. Murray's company posed on Culp's Hill, where the Confederate 2d Maryland had suffered so greatly and where local hero Murray had died.

By the 1880s, as proscriptions against Confederates were lifted and the war generation grew into middle age, Maryland swelled with a culture of Confederate nostalgia, part of a wave sweeping the South. The muster rolls of Confederate veterans' organizations grew, and Confederate voices found a literary market so eager that Union Marylanders were nearly overwhelmed. Bradley T. Johnson, who practiced law against John R. Kenly, wrote extensively about the war — Kenly kept his silence. McHenry Howard, perhaps shaken by wartime experiences, remained a quiet, private man, seldom venturing from his house in Baltimore or his estate in Western Maryland. But his memoirs, together with those of other colorful Maryland Confederates — the irrepressible Harry Gilmor and Henry Kyd Douglas — formed a body of lively, romantic Maryland Confederate wartime literature that outshone the dutiful regimental histories put forth by Union Marylanders.

In the spring of 1885 the "The Confederate Relief Bazaar Assocation of Maryland," composed of representatives from the Society of the Army and Navy of the Confederate States in the State of Maryland, the Association of the Maryland Line, and the Ladies' Confederate Memorial and Beneficial Association, held its first bazaar at the Fifth Regiment Armory in Baltimore. Generals Isaac Ridgway Trimble and Bradley T. Johnson worked on the finance committee, and Johnson's wife and Judge George William Brown, mayor of Baltimore in 1861, figured prominently on the board. Each state of

Above: "Gov. E. E. Jackson and Staff at the Dedication of the Maryland Monuments, Gettysburg, October 25, 1888." From Report of the State of Maryland Gettysburg Monument Commission, 1891. Below: Maryland Confederate veterans gathered at the monument to the 2d Maryland Infantry on Culp's Hill, Gettysburg Battlefield, in October, 1894. The regimental association had wanted the inscription on their monument, of granite from the quarries of Richard Snowden Andrews and dedicated eight years earlier, to read that they had charged from Rock Creek about 7 P.M. July 2, taken the line of Union works at this point, and held their position until the next morning. To their anger, the Gettysburg Memorial Association changed the proposed wording from "Charging" and "Capturing" to "Advancing" and "occupied," making it appear that the Confederates had been unopposed.

The Maryland monument, honoring every state unit that fought at the battle of Antietam, under construction near the Dunker church. It was dedicated on Memorial Day, 1900. Antietam National Battlefield files.

the Confederacy, with Kentucky and Missouri joining Maryland to represent the troubled border, offered delicacies and items for sale. Tables honored Robert E. Lee, Stonewall Jackson, and William Murray. The "Floral Temple," "Tent, with Gypsy Fortune Tellers," "Jacob's Well," and a lunch room raised $31,000 in economically hard times for the care of indigent Confederates and burial or memorialization of the dead.

The following year Maryland Confederates invaded Pennsylvania a second time. In 1864 Pennsylvania had chartered a Gettysburg Battlefield Memorial Association to preserve the now sacred ground as the armies had left it. In 1880, when only four monuments had been erected on the field, the G.A.R. took control from the local directors and created rules and guidelines by which monuments would be located and inscribed. As victors write the history, so the G.A.R. would write, or at least oversee, its inscription in granite and bronze.

Onto this field in August 1885 marched the aging men of the 2d Maryland with a request to erect a monument to their own on Culp's Hill. The Monument Association designated a former major and two sergeants to walk over the ground with the former Rebels to select the site. A skirmish broke out when the Marylanders located their monument where they insisted they had been, inside the Union works. This "important precedent"—the siting of a Rebel monument inside Union lines—prompted the major to call

for reinforcements. The executive committee decided to site the monument before the breastworks and alter the wording of their inscription. Whereas the Marylanders claimed they had "charged" from Rock Creek up the steep slopes and "taken the line of works" in their front, the inscription now read that they had "advanced" from the creek and "occupied" an abandoned line of works.

On November 19, 1886, with speeches and an escort from the 5th Maryland, two thousand Marylanders converged on Gettysburg to dedicate the 2d Maryland's monument, the first Confederate monument on the field. The celebration was subdued. Solemnly avoiding any Union or Confederate music, the 5th Maryland's band played only dirges.

Far grander was the scene two years later at the dedication of the Maryland Union monuments on Culp's Hill and in the Wheatfield. Gov. E. E. Jackson appeared with five thousand Marylanders and a half-mile long column of infantry: a dozen G.A.R. posts, the 5th Regiment, the Baltimore and Hagerstown Light Infantry regiments, the Linganore, Towson, and Bond Guards, the Veteran Volunteer Firemen of Baltimore, survivors of the five Maryland units involved at Gettysburg, and the Monumental City Guards and Baltimore Rifles— two "colored companies" from Baltimore "whose fine marching attracted much attention." With speeches and benedictions, they dedicated monuments on Culp's

The unveiling of the Confederate Monument, Baltimore, May 2, 1903. Facing page: Maj. Gen. Andrew C. Trippe delivering the opening address. The Confederacy had won many Marylanders' hearts, if not the war.

Although born in Baltimore, James Ryder Randall's career as a newspaper editor and poet kept him in the deep South for most of his life—in New Orleans, Alabama, and finally Augusta, Georgia. For two years in the late 1880s he served as chief editorial writer for the Baltimore American, but the relationship was not a happy one. Throughout his later life Randall made frequent visits to Baltimore, enjoying fame as the author of the poem and song that had made his state famous. Sadly, at the time of Randall's death at age sixty-nine in 1908, former governor Edwin Warfield had been working to create an office—"keeper of the archives"—that might enable the poet to spend his last days in comfort in the state he glorified. Upon his death there was public discussion about bringing Randall's body home for burial in Maryland, with a suitable monument to be erected, but he remains buried in Augusta. The state legislature ordered that a portrait be procured and hung in the old senate chamber in honor of the "poet and patriot, whose name will be forever held in kindly remembrance by all the citizens of our beloved State." "Maryland, My Maryland" was officially adopted as the State Song in 1939.

McHenry Howard, who witnessed some of the severest fighting of the war, as a young soldier (above) and a quiet, reclusive veteran near his Western Maryland estate (right).

After the war Gen. Felix Agnus (right) enjoyed a long career as business manager and later publisher of the Baltimore American. He was a popular speaker at veterans' reunions, both of the G.A.R. and the United Confederate Veterans. His Greenspring Valley mansion, "Nacirema," ("American" spelled backwards) later became the home of opera star Rosa Ponselle.

John Wesley Cole, a free black from Manchester, served with Co. F, 4th Regiment U.S.C.T. His family remembered that he took great pride in donning his old uniform and marching in parades with other local veterans. Historical Society of Carroll County.

Hill, where they had clashed with brothers and friends in Confederate gray, moving the Gettysburg *Compiler* to note: "There is an old saying that 'Maryland does everything like a gentleman.'"[5]

By the turn of the century, as the war generation grew into old age, their wounds had largely healed. The bitterness engendered by the nation's most terrible war was waning, even in this state which had seen its sons go forth to fight one another. On Memorial Day, 1900, symbolic of the general reconciliation, Marylanders dedicated on Antietam battlefield a perfect tribute in remembrance of a brothers' war — a monument to both sides. Orchestrated by a bi-partisan state commission (including former Confederate Henry Kyd Douglas and Union Col. Benjamin F. Taylor) and located near the Dunker Church on ground raked by Union and Confederate Maryland batteries, the Maryland monument honors every state unit involved on that terrible day in September, 1862.

Not everyone felt conciliatory. In May, 1903, thousands gathered in Baltimore's Mt. Royal Avenue for the unveiling of the Confederate Monument, presented by the United Daughters of the Confederacy. It was a glorious tribute to the Lost Cause that had finally cap-tured the city. Maj. Gen. Andrew Trippe, commander of the Maryland Division, United Confederate Veterans, introduced McHenry Howard, who recalled at defiant length the deeds and bravery of Maryland Confederates. Some years later a loving memorial to the sacrifices of Southern women arose on Charles Street north of Homewood.

In 1909, at the Mt. Royal Avenue entrance to Druid Hill Park, Baltimore finally erected a Union monument. The city hosted its last gathering of Union men with coolly paternalistic tolerance. "As the monument is the first memorial to be erected here to the Union soldiers and sailors of the Civil War," explained the *News-American*, "large delegations of veterans will be present and the space immediately in front of the monument, where the proceedings will be within easy reach of their fast failing eyes and ears, has been reserved for their especial benefit." A squad of extra police, the paper went on to say had been detailed "to see that the veterans come to no harm and also to take care that they find the places assigned to them."[6]

The only Union memorial in Baltimore was later moved to facilitate construction of an expressway.

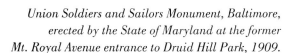

Union Soldiers and Sailors Monument, Baltimore, erected by the State of Maryland at the former Mt. Royal Avenue entrance to Druid Hill Park, 1909.

Notes

Slavery

1. Frederick Douglass, *Life and Times of Frederick Douglass* ([repr.] New York: Macmillan Publishing Company, 1962), p. 37 and passim.
2. William S. McFeely, *Frederick Douglass* (New York: W. W. Norton & Company, 1991), pp. 30–32.
3. Earl Conrad, *Harriet Tubman* (Washington, D.C.: Associated Publishers, 1943), p. 71.

Insurrection!

1. Material for this essay is drawn from Stephen B. Oates, *To Purge this Land with Blood: A Biography of John Brown* (New York: Harper & Row, 1970).

A Terrible Choice

1. B. F. Watson, *Addresses, Reviews and Episodes Chiefly Concerning the "Old Sixth" Massachusetts Regiment* (New York, 1901).
2. Lyman Van Buren Furber to his mother, 23 April 1861, Lyman Van Buren Furber Papers, MS 1450, Maryland Historical Society.
3. Hans L. Trefousse, *Ben Butler: The South Called Him Beast!* (New York: Twayne Publishers, 1957), p. 61.
4. Mark E. Neely, Jr., *The Fate of Liberty: Abraham Lincoln and Civil Liberties* (New York: Oxford University Press, 1991), p. 19.
5. Charles B. Clark, "Suppression and Control of Maryland, 1861–1865," *Maryland Historical Magazine*, 54 (1959): 260–61.

Brother Against Brother

1. Camper, 252]
2. James H. Bready, "Play Ball! The Legacy of Nineteenth-Century Baltimore Baseball," *Maryland Historical Magazine*, 87 (1992): p. 205.

Invasion . . . or Deliverance?

1. Stephen W. Sears, *Landscape Turned Red: The Battle of Antietam* (New Haven and New York: Ticknor & Fields, 1983), p. 73.
2. Ibid., p. 85.
3. Ibid., p. 113.

Antietam

1. John M. Priest, *Antietam: The Soldiers' Battle* (Shippensburg, Pa.: White Mane Publishing Co.), pp. 162, 169–70.
2. William Frassanito, *Antietam: The Photographic Legacy of America's Bloodiest Day*, pp. 128–29.
3. Ibid., pp. 178–85.

Freedom

1. Wagandt, "The Army Versus Maryland Slavery, 1862–1864," *Civil War History*, 10 (1964): 143.
2. Randall Jimerson, *The Private Civil War: Popular Thought During the Sectional Conflict* (Baton Rouge and London: Louisiana State University Press, 1988), pp. 96–97; New York *Tribune* cited in ibid., p. 105.
3. Quoted in Shelby Foote, *The Civil War: A Narrative* (3 vols; New York: Random House, Inc., 1974), 3:537.

Innocence Lost

1. Henry Kyd Douglas, *I Rode with Stonewall, Being chiefly the war experiences of the youngest member of Jackson's staff from the John Brown Raid to the hanging of Mrs. Surratt* (Chapel Hill: University of North Carolina Press, 1940), pp. 249–62.
2. MS 1834, Maryland Historical Society.
3. Harry Gilmor, *Four Years in the Saddle* (New York: Harper & Brothers, 1866), p. 178.

Point Lookout

1. Southern Literary Classics Series (Chapel Hill: University of North Carolina Press, 1969), p. 198.

2. Henry E. Shepherd, *Narrative of Prison Life at Baltimore and Johnson's Island, Ohio* (Baltimore: Commercial Ptg. & Sta. Co., 1917), p. 7; Charles T. Loehr, "Point Lookout; Address before Pickett Camp Confederate Veterans, October 10, 1890," *Southern Historical Society Papers*, 18 (1890): 115–16; Anthony M. Keiley, *In Vinculis, or, The Prisoner of War* (Petersburg, Va.: Daily Index Office, 1866), pp. 56–57; Benjamin P. Thomas and Harold M. Hyman, *Stanton: The Life and Times of Lincoln's Secretary of War* (New York: Alfred A. Knopf, 1962), pp. 372–73.
3. Excerpt from the diary of Bartlett Yancey Malone in Edwin W. Beitzell, *Point Lookout Prison Camp for Confederates* (published by the author, 1972), pp. 56–57; C. W. Jones, *In Prison at Point Lookout*, in ibid., p. 92; J. B. Traywick, "Prison Life at Point Lookout," *Southern Historical Society Papers*," 18 (1891): 432; Charles T. Loehr, "Point Lookout. Address before Pickett Camp Confederate Veterans, October 10, 1890," *Southern Historical Society Papers*, 18 (1890): 116; Keiley, *In Vinculis*, pp. 66–67; Beitzell, *Point Lookout*, p. 91.
4. The accounts of prisoners' mistreatment by guards at Point Lookout is almost uniformly bitter. See for example, Loehr, "Point Lookout," p. 118; N. F. Harman, "Prison Experiences at Point Lookout, Md.," *Confederate Veteran*, 15 (1907): 400; and the diaries of Bartlett Yancey Malone and Charles Warren Hutt in Beitzell, *Point Lookout*, and pp. 22ff. But the guards at other prisons behaved in much the same way. At Johnson's Island, "The sentinels availed themselves, with few exceptions, of every occasion to insult us and shoot." See Decimus et Ultimus Barziza, *The Adventures of a Prisoner of War, 1863–1864*, ed. by R. Henderson Schaffler (Austin: University of Texas Press, 1964), p. 78.
5. Diary of Charles Warren Hutt, August 11, 1864, in Beitzell, *Point Lookout*, p. 79. As is the case with many figures in the Civil War, the precise number of prisoners held at Point Lookout and the number who died is uncertain. This figure is taken from Beitzell, *Point Lookout*, p. 120.

The Final Tragedy

1. *The Lincoln Memorial* (New York: Bunce & Huntington, 1865), cited in Richard J. S. Gutman and Kellie O. Gutman, John Wilkes Booth Himself (Dover, Mass.: Hired Hand Press, 1979), p. 16.
2. Roy Z. Chamlee, Jr., *Lincoln's Assassins: A Complete Account of Their Capture, Trial, and Punishment* (Jefferson, N.C.: McFarland & Company, Inc., 1990), pp. 474–75.
3. Ibid., pp. 98–99, 476.
4. Virginia Lomax, *The Old Capitol and Its Inmates by a Lady* (New York: E. J. Hale and Co., 1867), p. 83, cited in Chamlee, *Lincoln's Assassins*, p. 92.
5. Thomas Reed Turner, *Beware the People Weeping: Public Opinion and the Assassination of Abraham Lincoln* (Baton Rouge: Louisiana State University Press, 1982), p. 50.

Remembrance

1. McFeely, *Frederick Douglass*, pp. 235–36. Douglass's other son, Charles, transferred from the 54th Mass. to the 5th Mass. Cavalry and was stationed at Pt. Lookout sometime between March and May 1864. He was discharged in September with a lung ailment (ibid., p. 230).
2. Paul H. Buck, *The Road to Reunion, 1865–1900*, Boston: Little, Brown and Company, 1937), p. 236ff.
3. G. Harrison Orians, "The Origins of the Ring Tournament in the United States," *Maryland HIstorical Magazine*, 36 (1941): 263–77.
4. Mary Ellen Thomsen, *Loudon Park Celebrating 125 Years* (Baltimore, 1979), p. 21.
5. October 30, 1888.
6. *News American*, May 30, 1909. The monument was later moved for expressway construction. It now stands in Wyman Park, on Charles Street in Baltimore.

Index

Virginian and ardent Confederate John Tabb enlisted aboard a blockade-runner early in the war. In June, 1864, he was captured and sent to Point Lookout prison. One day, while lying sick, he heard Sidney Lanier playing his flute on the other side of the camp. Tabb searched out Lanier and the two became fast friends and tentmates. Both eventually taught at the Johns Hopkins University — as far north as Tabb would go, for he refused ever to cross the Mason-Dixon Line — and played in the Peabody Orchestra in Baltimore. Lanier died in 1881. Years later, haunted by a melody Lanier had played frequently at Point Lookout, Tabb reproduced the tune for a friend, Edwin Litchfield Turnbull, and asked him to arrange it for piano. Called "The Melody from Lanier's Flute," the music made its way to the Peabody Orchestra, the Boston Symphony Orchestra, and the White House, where it was played by the U.S. Marine Corps band. From Father Tabb: His Life and Work (Boston: The Stratford Company, 1921).